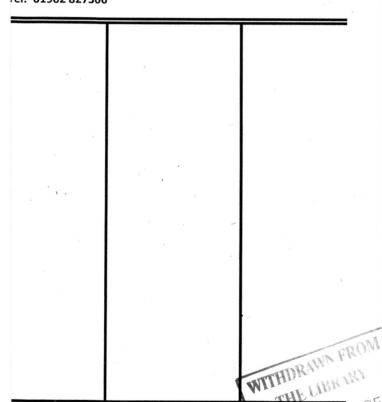

GIAMBATTISTA VICO

ON THE STUDY METHODS OF OUR TIME

TRANSLATED WITH AN
INTRODUCTION AND NOTES BY
ELIO GIANTURCO

PREFACE BY
DONALD PHILLIP VERENE

WITH A TRANSLATION OF
*The Academies and the Relation
between Philosophy and Eloquence*
BY DONALD PHILLIP VERENE

CORNELL UNIVERSITY PRESS

ITHACA AND LONDON

First published 1990 by Cornell University Press
First printing, Cornell Paperbacks, 1990

Library of Congress Cataloging-in-Publication Data

Vico, Giambattista, 1668–1744.
    [De nostri temporis studiorum ratione. English]
    On the study methods of our time / Giambattista Vico ; translated, with an introduction and notes, by Elio Gianturco ; preface by Donald Phillip Verene ; with a translation of The academies and the relation between philosophy and eloquence by Donald Phillip Verene.
    p. cm.
    Translation of: De nostri temporis studiorum ratione.
    Vico's oration translated from the Italian.
    Rev. and enl. version of the ed. published by Bobbs-Merrill, 1965, with new preface, appendix, and chronology of Vico's writings.
    Includes bibliographical references.
    ISBN-13: 978-0-8014-9778-0 (pbk. : alk. paper)
    1. Education, Higher. 2. Education—Philosophy. I. Vico, Giambattista, 1668-1744. Accademie e i rapporti tra la filosofia e l'eloquenza. English. 1990. II. Title.
LB575.V5D413   1990
370'.1—dc20   90-55226

CONTENTS

Preface   ix
  by Donald Phillip Verene

Translator's Introduction   xxi
  by Elio Gianturco

Chronology of Vico's Principal Writings   xlvii

Note on the Text   xlix

ON THE STUDY METHODS
OF OUR TIME

I.   3

Subject of the present discourse: the comparison, not of the various branches of learning, but of the study methods of our time and of antiquity. What factors make up every method of study? Distribution of the topics to be discussed, new instruments of the sciences. New aids to studies. Which is, today, the aim of our studies?

II.   9

Advantages of our study methods that derive from the instruments used by modern sciences. Advantages of philosophical criticism. Analysis. Introduction of the geometrical method into physics; of chemistry into medicine. Pharmaceutical chemistry. The introduction of chemistry into physics, and of mechanics into medicine. The microscope. The telescope. The mariner's compass. Introduction of modern geometry and physics into mechanics. Advantages accruing to us from the use of new devices: reduction to theoretical precepts of matters pertaining to human discretion in the conduct of life. Masterpieces of art. Printing. Universities. Advantages deriving from the aim we have in view in our studies.

III. 12

Drawbacks of modern criticism. Criticism injurious to prudence. Criticism an obstacle to eloquence: it hinders the arts, which thrive on imagination, memory, or both. How the ancients obviated the drawbacks of modern criticism. Modern neglect of *topics,* i.e., the art of forms of arguments employed in probable reasoning, to the benefit of criticism. Drawbacks of this neglect. How the disadvantages inherent in philosophical criticism may be avoided.

IV. 21

Drawbacks caused by the introduction of the geometrical method into physics. It kills the desire to explore nature further. How we can study physics as philosophers, namely, as Christian philosophers. The use of the geometrical method impairs the faculty to express oneself tastefully and with acuteness. It forms an obstacle to free and ample utterance. It generates a sluggish diction, to be avoided as much as possible in eloquence. How its drawbacks may be obviated.

V. 26

Analysis. It may be useless to mechanics. How the disadvantages of analysis can be avoided.

VI. 30

Drawbacks of our modern method of studying and practicing medicine. How to remove them.

VII. 33

Disadvantages of our modern study methods in the fields of ethics, civil doctrine, and eloquence, from the viewpoint of the purpose at which we aim. Civil doctrine. Eloquence. Civil doctrine and eloquence again. How the drawbacks of our study methods may be remedied in regard to the guiding principles of the conduct of life, and in the domain of eloquence.

VIII. 41

Poetry. Under what conditions the modern critical procedure is useful to poetry. Suitability of the geometrical method to poetry.

"Ideal" or "universal" truth is the proper guiding principle of poetry. Study of modern physics is conducive to poetry.

IX.   44

Christian theology.

X.   46

Disadvantages of preceptive handbooks framing rules on matters that pertain to the practical conduct of life. How to eliminate these disadvantages.

XI.   47

The practice and study of law. Greek jurisprudence. Roman jurisprudence. Jurisprudence of the free Roman republic. Jurisprudence under the Emperors, prior to Hadrian. Jurisprudence under Hadrian. Under Constantine. Advantages and drawbacks of the study of law. First advantage and first drawback; second advantage, second drawback; third advantage, third drawback; fourth advantage, fourth drawback; fifth advantage, fifth drawback; sixth advantage, sixth drawback tentatively expressed. Advantage of the jurisprudential method of Accursius and of his disciples. Its drawbacks: first and second. How disadvantages in the study of law may be avoided.

XII.   70

Masterpieces of art. What drawbacks their existence produces. How these drawbacks may be got rid of.

XIII.   72

Typographical characters. The disadvantages of printing. How they may be overcome.

XIV.   74

Universities. Their drawbacks; how they may be remedied.

XV.   77

Conclusion.

Appendix: The Academies and the Relation   83
    between Philosophy and Eloquence
    Translated by Donald Phillip Verene

PREFACE

When Elio Gianturco published his translation of *On the Study Methods of Our Time* in 1965, the current renaissance in Vico studies among English-speaking scholars had not yet begun. The translations of Vico's *Autobiography* and *New Science* by Max Harold Fisch and Thomas Goddard Bergin had appeared in the 1940s, but they were not widely read. In English-language scholarship and especially in the world of Anglo-American philosophy, Vico was largely unknown; at most his name was associated with the beginnings of the philosophy of history. Followers of the literature of Hegelian idealism knew something of him through Benedetto Croce's *Aesthetic* (1909; 2d rev. ed. 1922) and R. G. Collingwood's *Idea of History* (1946). Scholars of modern political history as well as many general readers first encountered Vico's name in the opening section of Edmund Wilson's *To the Finland Station* (1940). Students of James Joyce's work became aware of Vico through Samuel Beckett's early essay "Dante. . . Bruno. Vico. . Joyce" (1929) and Joyce's own use of Vico in *Finnegans Wake* (1939).

The first systematic study of Vico in English is Robert Flint's *Vico*, published in 1884, and it still holds its own as a good book. During the first half of the twentieth century some scholarly writings appearing in English took note of Vico, but he was not a thinker who figured in the intellectual climate at large. One work that deserves mention, H. P. Adams's *Life and Writings of Giambattista Vico* (1935), however, offered a reliable picture of a thinker whose works did not yet exist in English. In Italy there has been a continuous literature on Vico, including various modern editions and collections of his works, a comprehensive picture of which can be gained from Croce's two-volume *Bibliografia vichiana* (revised and enlarged by Fausto Nicolini in 1947–48) and its supplements by Maria Donzelli (1973) and Andrea Battistini (1983). Vico has always been regarded as an important figure in the history of Italian philosophy. Since the late eighteenth and early nineteenth centuries, schools of Italian thought have developed their own interpretations of the significance of Vico's thought. The history of Italian philosophy of the modern period, however, is largely a self-contained affair that is only very selectively studied as part of the history of philosophy as understood by Northern Europeans and the Anglo-American world.

Fisch and Bergin's learned translations of the *Autobiography* and the *New Science* provided the foundation necessary for English-language studies. The initial step in the development of the current tradition of critical literature in English on Vico were Isaiah Berlin's lectures, "The Philosophical Ideas of Giambattista Vico," given in the late 1950s at the Italian Cultural Institute in London. Although these were published in specialized form, they did not become widely known until Berlin revised them as the Vico half of his *Vico and Herder* (1970). Yet in these lectures and in other places before the appearance of *Vico and Herder*, Berlin showed scholars that Vico was an original thinker of the first order, not simply an obscure figure of Italian thought whose chief claim to fame was as a precursor of other ideas.

Although Berlin connects Vico to another thinker, Herder, in his later book, his direct approach to the significance of Vico's ideas in his original lectures was a turning point in Vico studies, helping to free Vico from the bonds of Croce's desire to perceive Vico as the Italian Hegel. The separation of Vico's ideas from the tradition of Hegelianism, effected by English-speaking scholars and by Italian scholars such as Pietro Piovanni, was a necessary step in beginning the current renaissance in Vico studies; scholars needed to allow Vico's ideas to become flexible and attain their full range of possibilities within many different traditions and fields of thought. Many commentators now simply dismiss Croce's

Hegelian interpretation of Vico; I do not wish to advocate this dismissal. Croce's *La filosofia di Giambattista Vico*, published in 1911 and translated into English by Collingwood in 1913, is an extremely intelligent and valuable work, very much worth the contemporary reader's time. The work by the American Crocean Robert Caponigri, *Time and Idea: The Theory of History in Giambattista Vico*, published in 1953, though quite obscurely written, in many ways served to keep Vico alive for English-speaking scholars, at least as a figure about whom a whole book could be written. Arthur Child's monograph *Making and Knowing in Hobbes, Vico, and Dewey* was published the same year as Caponigri's work. Child's and several other small works appeared nearly in isolation.

Gianturco, who died in 1987, was among other things an authority on Italian philosophy and literature and the history of jurisprudence, and he took a philosophically non-doctrinaire approach to Vico's thought, as can be seen from the erudite translator's introduction in this edition. As Gianturco explains, the work translated here is the seventh oration of a series of inaugural orations that Vico delivered as part of the requirements of his position at the University of Naples. He wrote these inaugural orations, as he did all of his first works, in Latin. The *Autobiography* and the first and second versions of the *New Science* were written in Italian. The seventh oration, delivered in 1708 and published in 1709, *De nostri temporis studiorum ratione*, is widely regarded as the first statement of Vico's original philosophical position as well as a treasure-house of educational ideas.

Some scholars assume a more radical break between the first six orations and the seventh than is actually there. The first six are certainly much shorter and do not present the new theory of knowledge present in the seventh. Yet they should not be underestimated, as they contain some of Vico's basic themes. For example, the first oration's discussion of the generation of the gods and heroes from the faculty of *phantasia* as a fundamental power of thought is a theme retained and developed into the theory of "poetic wisdom" in the *New Science*. Vico's views in the sixth oration concerning the order of studies, the importance of the powers of memory and imagination in children, and the weakening of imagination as reasoning power grows stronger are themes that lead to those of the *De nostri*, where he revises and places them in terms of his new conception of knowledge. Gianturco's introduction ably introduces the text of the *De nostri* and I shall not attempt to add to it here except to comment on how he has rendered the title.

For the reader who does not grasp the meaning of Vico's title from the Latin, Gianturco's rendering of *De nostri temporis studiorum ratione* as "On the Study Methods of Our Time" may not successfully convey Vico's statement of his theme. The problem is with the term "study methods," the shortened title by which this work has come to be called in English. The genitive plural "*studiorum*" of the original title should be rendered as the English plural "studies." "*Ratione*" should be the singular "method" in English, not the plural "methods." Thus one might more literally think of these key terms of Vico's Latin title as just the reverse of Gianturco's rendering—not "study methods," but "method of studies." The idea of *ratio* is difficult to render. *Ratio* has a fairly wide number of meanings stemming from the idea of a reckoning, account, or computation; it can signify a plan, scheme, system, method, or order. Vico's title has more the sense of the drawing-up of an order of studies according to some criterion than of the presentation of a method of thought in the modern sense of the term.

For the modern reader method has come to imply how to do something, a procedure, steps or action necessary to take in order to achieve some desired result. This connotation shows how far the Cartesian sense of method has entered our understanding of the term. Vico's sense of method is not Descartes', nor is Vico interested in what would today be understood as "educational methods." As he points out in the first part of the oration, he wishes to weigh the Ancients against the Moderns in an attempt to discover a balance in their approaches to knowledge. He holds that studies should be introduced to cultivate first the powers of memory and imagination in the young and that too early an emphasis on the mastery of philosophical criticism and logic will make the mind sterile. The sense of wisdom and eloquence found in the Ancients should not be easily thrown over for the rapid assimilation of the techniques of modern invention and science. The arguments and ingenuities of the Moderns should be mastered, but only by mature minds that have been educated in the art of topics.

In the first part of his autobiography, that written in 1725, however, Vico uses the term "method" to refer to the *De nostri*, calling this oration that "of the method of study" (*"del metodo di studiare"*). His use here suggests a deliberate opposition to Descartes' *"méthode"* of the *Discours*, an opposition which parallels that which Vico wishes to institute between the genuine *storia* of his *Vita* showing the genesis and "causes both natural and moral" of his intellectual development and the feigned *histoire* that Descartes offers of himself in the *Discours*. Thus we are not wrong to think of Vico's title as involving "method." But if we consider the root sense of *ratio*, we might understand the title of Vico's work best as "On the System of Studies of Our Time." Because the present volume is a reissue of Gianturco's original translation and because for better or for worse the work has come to be known in English by Gianturco's title, I have not changed the title. I doubt that this poses any serious problem for readers so long as they keep the above comments in mind when approaching the work.

My criticisms of the title do not imply a dissatisfaction with Gianturco's translation of the text. Some may prefer a more literal statement at various places according to their own interpretive interests, but Gianturco's eloquent rendering of the full text conveys much of Vico's spirit. Translations of selections from several sections of the *De nostri* have been available in Leon Pompa's *Vico: Selected Writings*, published in 1982, but Gianturco's translation has been out of print for many years and is not always found even in many academic libraries. It is a pleasure to have it available once again for students of Vico.

The current renaissance in Vico studies began in 1968, the tercentenary of Vico's birth. That year the American quarterly of Italian studies, *Forum Italicum*, published a special issue in honor of Vico, with numerous articles by leading scholars assessing his importance. In that same year similar publications appeared in Italy, such as *Omaggio a Vico*, published in Naples. The celebration continued with the publication one year later of a comprehensive volume of forty-one essays by scholars from all fields of the humanities and social sciences and from many countries, titled *Giambattista Vico: An International Symposium*. This volume was the brainchild of Giorgio Tagliacozzo, who organized it over a period of years and served as its editor, with Hayden White as coeditor. The "symposium" of the subtitle did not occur in any place beyond the pages of the volume itself. The contributors—Ernesto Grassi, Yvon Belaval, René Wellek, Edmund Leach, H. Stuart Hughes, Berlin, Gillo Dorfles, Herbert Read, and others—met only through their essays in the book, but the range of the essays and the prominence of their authors demonstrated the relevance and importance of Vico to various fields of thought. Gianturco contributed an essay on Vico's significance in the history of legal thought and served as one of the consulting editors of the volume.

In 1976 a second volume, *Giambattista Vico's Science of Humanity*, appeared. Edited by Tagliacozzo and myself, it contains twenty-eight essays and a first translation into English by Bergin and Fisch of Vico's "Practic of the New Science" (now appended to the current paperback edition of the *New Science*). A third volume, *Vico and Contemporary Thought* (1979), edited by Tagliacozzo, Michael Mooney, and myself, contains essays and comments by thirty-six scholars from many fields on various aspects of Vico's thought in relation to contemporary problems. These papers originated at a conference held in New York in 1976, sponsored by the Institute for Vico Studies, the New School for Social Research, and Columbia University.

In 1978 an international conference in Venice commemorated the 250th anniversary of the first appearance of Vico's *Autobiography*. From this conference Tagliacozzo gathered thirty-six selected essays in his volume *Vico: Past and Present* (1981), and two more volumes of the papers from the conference appeared in Italian: *Vico oggi* (1979), edited by Andrea Battistini, and *Vico e Venezia* (1982), edited by Cesare de Michelis and Gilberto Pizzamiglio. Tagliacozzo later edited a volume of original essays titled *Vico and Marx: Affinities and Contrasts* (1983). In 1987 I edited *Vico and Joyce*, a selection of papers presented at a week-long international conference on these two authors, which was held in Venice in the summer of 1985 at the Cini Foundation.

The center for much of this consistent and intense international attention to Vico is the Institute for Vico Studies, founded by Tagliacozzo in 1974 in New York and now affiliated with Emory University in Atlanta. Representative of the widespread interest in Vico was the Institute's founding in 1983 of the annual *New Vico Studies*. Together with the Italian annual *Bollettino del Centro di Studi vichiani* founded in 1971, *New Vico Studies* documents the ongoing work on Vico. The past two decades have also seen a number of book-length studies on Vico's thought from various perspectives among English-speaking scholars—Frederick Vaughan's *The Political Philosophy of Giambattista Vico* (1972), Pompa's *Vico* (1975; 2d ed. 1990), Berlin's above-mentioned *Vico and Herder* (1976), my own *Vico's Science of Imagination* (1981), Mooney's *Vico in the Tradition of Rhetoric* (1985), Peter Burke's *Vico* (1985), Bruce Haddock's *Vico's Political Thought* (1986), Gino Bedani's *Vico Revisited* (1989), and Ernesto Grassi's *Vico and Humanism* (1990). Tagliacozzo provides a detailed picture of much of this development in his series "Toward a History of Anglo-American Vico Scholarship," which has appeared in issues of *New Vico Studies*. Full references to these works and a general picture of the extant lit-

erature on and citations to Vico in English appear in *A Bibliography of Vico in English 1884–1984*, published in 1986 in
the series of bibliographies by the Philosophy Documenta-
tion Center and in annual supplements published in *New
Vico Studies*.

I do not intend with these remarks to give a full picture of
this renaissance of interest in Vico, not even of that in English, and I have made no attempt to describe publications in
Italian and other languages. There are, for example, the
translations of Vico's *Autobiography* and the *De nostri* into
French by Alain Pons (1981) and of the *New Science* into German by Vittorio Hösle and Christoph Jermann (1990). The
widespread interest in Vico is not limited to American and
European scholars. Translations of the *New Science* have appeared in Japanese (1979) and Chinese (1987). No such interest existed when Gianturco published his translation in
1965, just before this new energy of Vico studies began to
take shape. This renaissance occurred because of a shift in
the way in which scholars regarded Vico's thought. To the
extent that Vico was known two decades ago, it was for his
cyclic view of history—that history proceeds through *corsi*
and *ricorsi*. The new interest in Vico, which stemmed from
Berlin's lectures on Vico's philosophical ideas, turned attention to the views of human knowledge which are present in
Vico's works, principally in the *New Science*. These views center on Vico's conceptions of historical knowledge, of the
imagination and memory, the unity of knowledge, the development of mind, and of rhetoric and learning. This focus on
his views of knowledge has allowed scholars from all fields of
the humanities and the social sciences to relate their work to
Vico, making him a source figure in many new areas.

The time has also become ripe for a conception of human
knowledge, history, and the human condition that is oppo-
site to the one derived from Descartes and different from
what one finds in the traditions of German philosophy.
Vico's work provides this alternative. He appears to current
thinkers almost as a contemporary figure from whose ideas

they can draw new intellectual breath because he does not come to us from any of the somewhat exhausted traditions of rationalism, empiricism, or idealism. In this seventh oration he takes his first strong step to oppose Descartes and Cartesianism, even though he offers no direct discussion of Descartes in it. He published his direct criticism of Descartes' conception of knowledge and truth the year after *De nostri*, in *De antiquissima Italorum sapientia* (1710), a work that now appears in its first full English translation, by Lucia M. Palmer, and includes the *Risposte*. One can read it with profit alongside this oration to gain a full view of how Vico begins his philosophy as a response to Cartesianism.

The *De nostri* is Vico's first statement of his original philosophical position formulated as a conception of human education. It stands as the only short work that can be employed as an introduction to his philosophy. The *New Science*, the main work of Vico's philosophy, is a large and difficult book; it requires a smaller work to serve as an introduction. The *De nostri* is that work. In the third paragraph of his introduction Gianturco points out that Vico's oration of 1732, *De mente heroica* ("On the Heroic Mind"), may be considered the logical prolongation of the *De nostri*. A translation of this oration by Elizabeth Sewell and Anthony C. Sirignano appears in the above-mentioned volume *Vico and Contemporary Thought*, and can also be found in the journal *Social Research* 43, no. 4 (1976).

I have appended to this volume my translation of what might be considered Vico's last philosophical statement. In the standard edition of Vico's works Nicolini gave this the title "Le accademie e i rapporti tra la filosofia e l'eloquenza" (*The Academies and the Relation between Philosophy and Eloquence*). Vico delivered this oration to the Academy of Oziosi, one of the learned societies of Naples, in 1737, eight years before his death. Although he was revising the text of his second version of the *New Science* at his death, this short oration remains as his last public statement and, like his original six and famous seventh orations, it concerns the notion of learning. It appears in English for the first time here, and although it has gone unnoticed by many Vico scholars, it reaffirms a number of interesting themes. Scholars may consider this oration, the *De nostri*, and the *De mente heroica* as a kind of trilogy in which Vico presents the full range of his most essential educational ideas.

The *De mente heroica* insists that education should allow the student to comprehend the "three worlds"—of things human, things natural, and things eternal—and that each field of study should be approached in terms of how it stands together with the whole of knowledge. Vico's reference to these three worlds of learning echoes the three worlds of nations, nature, and minds and God, which are depicted in his frontispiece to the *New Science* and which, he says at the end of his explanation of the frontispiece, represent the order in which the human minds of gentile peoples have been raised from earth to heaven. The incorporation of this threefold distinction in the *De mente heroica* suggests that the whole of his philosophy can be seen as a conception of the education of the human soul.

This oration to the Academy of Oziosi reflects Vico's views on wisdom, the unity of knowledge, and the importance of rhetoric found in the *De nostri* and the *De mente heroica*. It adds to Vico's views on the education of the young his views on the mutual education of accomplished scholars. It is a plea for scholars to operate as a true community and not to separate rhetoric and eloquence from knowledge. For the contemporary reader it is a plea to strike out against the problem of the fragmentation of knowledge and the development of the technical sense of knowledge to the detriment of the promotion of knowledge as a whole. As Vico proclaims in the *De nostri*, "The whole is really the flower of wisdom," and he adds, in his oration to the Academy of Oziosi, "Eloquence is none other than wisdom speaking."

My translation of Vico's address to the Academy of Oziosi here replaces the extended bibliography in Gianturco's original edition. The picture of the literature that Gianturco's original bibliography presents has been superseded by bibliographies readily available elsewhere.

In the new Vico literature one of the least-examined aspects of Vico's thought and one of its most creative aspects are his views on human education. One of the pioneers in calling attention to this aspect is my colleague Giorgio Tagliacozzo. I thank him for his efforts behind the scenes in rescuing this edition of one of Vico's most important works from its out-of-print status. Perhaps its *ricorso* will offer new impetus for exploring further this part of Vico's treasure-house.

DONALD PHILLIP VERENE

Atlanta, Georgia
May 1990

TRANSLATOR'S INTRODUCTION

We live in a Cartesian world, a world of scientific research, technology, and gadgets, which invade and condition our lives; of new disciplines, like kybernetics, sociometry, biometry; of new machines, like electronic computers, videos, satellites. To our physical milieu might fitly be applied the designation which Balthazar Bekker, a Dutch author who influenced Fontenelle, affixed to one of his books, *De betooverde Weereld* (1691–1693)—the magical (or "hexed up") world. In our milieu, so intensely penetrated on one hand by mathematical intellectualism, by science-worship, and, on the other, by an exacting pragmatic utilitarianism, the inevitable outcome has been the downgrading of the humanistic disciplines. A pessimist might say that we are witnessing the ultimate reduction of the prestige that the *humaniora* formerly held, both in learned circles and among the general public, with consequences that are plainly visible in the educational curriculum and in the criteria governing our young men's choice of profession.

Whatever can be said to defend and vindicate the humanities has already been set forth by able pleaders, especially in America and England. But fully to understand the issues involved, it is not superfluous to go back to the early-modern origins of the debate *scientism versus humanism*. That debate, from which the idea of progress was to emerge in full éclat, arose as an offshoot of the Quarrel of the Ancients and the Moderns, which took place in the seventeenth and eighteenth centuries in France, England, and Italy, concerning the comparative merits of classical and modern culture. Of this discussion, a most important fruit was G. B. Vico's *De nostri temporis studiorum ratione,* which is presented here in English translation for the first time.

In compliance with a custom at the University of Naples that the professor of rhetoric deliver the address solemnizing the opening of each new school year, Vico, who had been the incumbent of that professorship since 1698, was invited in 1708 to give the "inaugural" speech at that ceremony, to which the presence of the Viceroy of Naples and of Cardinal Vincenzo Grimani lent particular luster. As his topic, Vico chose to compare the study methods of classical antiquity with those of his epoch. He revised and enlarged the address in 1709, and it was printed in that year at the University's expense. It is the seventh in the series of his "inaugurals," the six preceding having been delivered during the period from October 18, 1699, to October 18, 1707. The *De nostri* is the only one that was deemed worthy of appearing in print: it is the most outstanding of Vico's academic productions, and epitomizes his educational ideas. (Additional light is shed on these ideas in Chapter Three of his *Autobiography*, 1725, and by two items in his *Correspondence,* letters to Abbé Esperti and Father de Vitry, both dated 1726.) Vico's last inaugural, his eighth, in 1732, entitled *De mente heroica* (*The Heroic Mind*), may be considered the logical prolongation of the *De nostri*. It is one of the most inspired "invitations to learning" ever penned, a scintillating paean in praise of what Goethe would have called the Faustian impulse toward encyclopedic knowledge. The *eros* of learning has seldom been expressed in more electrifying terms.

In its homeland, Vico's *De nostri,* perhaps the most brilliant defense of the humanities ever written, has for some decades now held the rank of an educational "classic." Fausto Nicolini, the *doyen* of Vico studies, aptly underlines its significance by pointing out that "it is the most important pedagogic essay between Locke's *Thoughts on Education* (1693) and the *Émile* (1762) of Rousseau." Seven translations into modern Italian, one into Spanish, one into German, one into Polish, and a partial one into French (by no less a person than Jules Michelet, the greatest French Romantic historian) attest to the high regard in which it is held in continental Europe and in Latin America.

As for England (aside from an appreciation contained in Robert Flint's old monograph on Vico) and the English-speaking world in general, *habent sua fata libelli:* the *De nostri* is conspicuously absent (so far as I know) from all histories of education and educational thought (many of them otherwise excellent) written by English and American scholars. Yet the *De nostri* should have been of prime interest to historians raised in the Anglo-Saxon cultural tradition, for it is probably the most signal example in the European eighteenth century, besides the French *Encyclopédie,* of a work directly inspired by Francis Bacon. Vico declares his indebtedness to the great *Verulamius* in the opening paragraphs. We have no history of the impact of Bacon's thought upon eighteenth-century Italy; but when it comes to be written, Vico's *De nostri* will loom unmistakably large.[1] I may add that Bacon's influence is also present in Vico's *Oratio V,* and in the *Scienza Nuova* (*The New Science*), where Bacon's method is transferred from the study of nature to that of society and history.

There is another reason why the *De nostri* should have been of interest to scholars sharing the English intellectual tradition. The *De nostri,* as Rigault noticed, sets the seal of a philosophical conclusion upon the Quarrel of the Ancients and the Moderns. Vico draws, so to speak, the final balance-sheet of the great controversy; not only that, but transposes it to a

---

[1] It will also be seen that the other eighteenth-century Italian essay of truly European range, Cesare Beccaria's *Dei delitti e delle pene* (*On Crimes and Punishments*), 1764, which brought about a far-reaching revolution in the theory and practice of criminal law during and after the period of Enlightenment, is another document of that pervasive influence.

Perhaps the reason for the absence of the *De nostri* from all histories of education written in English is extremely simple: no English translation has been available. With an English translation of Beccaria's treatise now available (New York: Liberal Arts Press, Inc., 1963), it seems imperative to companion it with a translation of Vico's educational masterpiece.

ground where the problem posited can receive a solution. He is a reconciler of the two factions; he lifts their debate to a high philosophical plane, he rises to the concept of a modern culture harmonizing the scientific with the humanistic aspects of education.

There is, finally, a special point of attraction for Anglo-Saxon scholars. In England, as the researches of Professor R. Foster Jones have established, the Quarrel, which in France revolved around matters almost exclusively literary, becomes definitely oriented toward the sciences (in this, Bacon's influence is apparent). It became a battle between conservatism and progress in the scientific domain. The reader of the *De nostri* cannot help noticing Vico's interest, not only in the humanities, eloquence, psychology, and literature, but also in mathematics, the natural sciences, and technology. In other words, his interests are richer and more complex than that of the French *littérateurs* (with the exception of Fontenelle); they lie much closer to the English than to the French pattern of discussion of the themes treated by the Quarrel.

Seldom, in the soberly reflective literature on that *venerabilis inceptor* of modern philosophy, Descartes, do we come across such a lyrical, vibrant exaltation of his intellectual eminence as we find in Damiron's *Essai sur l'histoire de la philosophie en France au XVIIe siècle* (Paris, 1846). You may dismiss simply as a patch of purple prose the following passage; nevertheless, it cogently describes the hegemonic sway of Descartes over the thought of his age. Descartes is the major planet of the philosophical firmament of his day:

> See how, around him, everything feels its power! Toward him there gravitate, although in different relationships, and each with its own glory, Malebranche, Spinoza, Leibniz, and all those who, devoting themselves less expressly to philosophical pursuits, nevertheless are great philosophical minds, like Arnauld, the men of Port Royal, Bossuet, and Fénelon. Likewise, there gravitate toward him, although to oppose him, Hobbes and Gassendi. Everything, during the seventeenth century, rotates

around Descartes: he is the vivifying planet of that intellectual firmament.[1]

All in all, Descartes was indeed the vivifying sun of the seventeenth century. But at the opening of the eighteenth century, there was another planet, who felt, it is true, the puissant influence of that central sun of the intellectual sky, but set out on an orbit of his own, its impetus leading him to still unexplored reaches of another firmament of ideas. His name was Giambattista Vico (1668–1744). His formative years stand in a polemical relationship to the thinker whom, with admiring antagonism, with a pride based on a consciousness of intellectual independence, he calls "Renato."

Vico's anti-Cartesianism first appears in the *De nostri*, in a form which is as sharp-edged as it is "clear and distinct" (a Cartesian anti-Cartesianism, so to speak). The next book, *De Antiquissima Italorum Sapientia (On the Very Ancient Wisdom of the Italians)*, marks an extension of that polemic (the *cogito*, for instance, receives a devastating treatment). What were the reasons for Vico's antagonism to Descartes?

One assumption must be discarded at the outset. The reasons were not nationalistic. The reading of Vico in a nationalistic key, in the manner of Gioberti, is unhistorical. In 1708, the date of the *De nostri*, the Kingdom of Naples, after a period of Spanish rule, was under Austrian domination; no idea of Italian chauvinism existed there, even phantasmally. Naples was a part of politically fragmented Italy, a "purely geographical expression" in Metternich's sense. Vico's *De Antiquissima* with its invention of a very ancient, deeply autochthonous "wisdom" (*sapientia*) is the embodiment of a myth,

[1] Only the inclusion of Malebranche into the pleiad of his outright satellites needs a certain qualification in the light of the remarks of Blondel, and also in view of the fact that, as René Dugas has shown, Malebranche controverts the Cartesian laws concerning the impact of physical bodies. Notice, also, the omission of Pascal and the misrepresentation of Leibniz, about whose anti-Cartesianism we are vastly enlightened by the recent, rich book of Yvon Belaval, *Leibniz critique de Descartes* (559 pp.; Paris: Gallimard, 1960).

which later inspired Vincenzo Cuoco, but was controverted by Foscolo, Dèlfico, and Micali. In the last analysis it reveals not political nationalism, but cultural pride.

What Vico dislikes, what he combats in Descartes, is not the overweeningness (the *boria*) of a thinker belonging to a different nation (and there would have been a measure of excuse for this attitude, in view of Descartes' depreciatory attitude toward Galileo, whose discoveries he considered as either erroneous or trivial), but "Renato's" professed antipathy, nay, utter contempt, for the *litterae humaniores,* and pre-eminently for languages.[2]

In order to understand the animus and the historical context of Vico's polemical thrusts against Descartes, a certain familiarity with the major streams of Cartesian criticism is necessary. Let me say at the outset that Vico's interpretation of Descartes' achievement is not unique; it is identical with the views of such eminent French critics as Louis Liard, Hamelin, Charles Adam, L. Brunschvicg, and Pierre Boutroux. (The latter's opinion as to the significance of the Cartesian analytic geometry completely coincides with that of Vico.[3])

[2] Corsano, therefore, goes too far when he asserts that the strongest expression of gallophobia prior to Alfieri's *Misogallo* is the excursus on the French language presented in the *De nostri.*

[3] "Brunschvicg deems that, subsequent to the *Rules,* Descartes became oriented toward a complete *intellectualization* of mathematics. See 'Mathématiques et métaphysique chez Descartes,' *Revue de métaphysique et de morale* (1927), p, 280; and *Les étapes de la pensée mathématique"* (Roger Lefèvre, *La vocation de Descartes* [Paris: Presses Universitaires, 1956], p. 147, note 1). Pierre Boutroux' analogous position is set forth in his *L'idéal scientifique des mathématiciens* (Paris: Presses Universitaires, 1955), as well as in his *L'imagination et les mathématiques selon Descartes* (Paris: F. Alcan, 1900), where we find this statement: "If we consider the whole of his scientific works, we see that Descartes is principally concerned with eliminating every notion addressing the imagination, and with reducing everything to the analytical ideas of pure understanding" (p. 19). It is unknown to me whether Brunschvicg and Boutroux knew of the identical view of Vico on this matter; if they did not, the coincidence of their opinions, and Vico's sharpness in emphasizing this aspect of the Cartesian analysis, are all the more striking.

On the immediate and long-range developments of Descartes' analytical

There are, roughly, two main kinds of Cartesian exegesis. I quote from Professor A. Carlini's *Il problema di Cartesio:*

> The debates which arose in times subsequent to the Cartesian age are still the same as those which came to the surface at that epoch. They follow two principal trends. One trend emphasizes Descartes' theological aspect, his role as a reformer of Scholastic (or, rather, Thomistic) metaphysics, and, on this point, this trend places Cartesian thought in connection with the resurgent Augustinianism of the seventeenth century. The other trend chooses to emphasize the epistemological aspect, to emphasize Descartes' position in the history of science, and focusses its interest solely upon the grandiose movement of research in the field of the physical sciences, which culminates in the physics of Newton. The first trend gives primary consideration to Descartes' *Meditations;* the other strongly underlines his *Principles of Philosophy.*[4]

The second trend gives primary place to Descartes' scientific methodology, as in the *Rules for the Direction of the Mind* and the *Discourse on Method.* Vico's *De nostri* evinces a close familiarity with the *Discourse,* which it attempts to refute step by step. Consequently, the *De nostri* is most intelligible to readers who have thoroughly assimilated the substance of the *Discourse* and that of the *Rules.*

Vico's originality in the history of anti-Cartesianism manifests itself in five points. The first is Vico's dissent from Descartes' view of the *Discourse* as a method of invention. The second is Vico's opposition to Descartes' methodological monism (Pascal had already voiced this opposition). The third is Vico's endeavor to demonstrate the superiority of "synthetic" or Euclidian geometry over Cartesian, analytical geometry. The fourth is the attempt to expose the weakness of Cartesian medicine and cosmology, and to declare the inadmissibility of the reduction of physics to mathematics. (One of the most

---

method, see Roger Lefèvre, *La vocation de Descartes,* pp. 148–149; Paul Tannery, *Notions de mathématique* (Paris: Delagrave, 1903), p. 342; and Jacques Chevalier, *Descartes* (Paris: Plon, 1921), p. 120.

4 A. Carlini, *Il problema di Cartesio* (Bari: Laterza, 1948); see pp. 25–27.

persistent of Cartesian "themes" is the mathematization of physics.) Finally—and this is the aspect that establishes the characteristic note of Vico's criticism of Descartes within the history of anti-Cartesianism—we have Vico's emphasis on man as an integrality (not sheer rationality, not merely intellect, but also fantasy, passion, emotion), and his insistence on the *historical and social dimension*. The vindication of the *historical dimension* of man is Vico's point of greatest originality, as Michelet very clearly perceived. In the *De nostri*, this comes to the fore in the section devoted to legal studies. I would not hesitate to call this part the earliest manifesto of *Juridical historicism*. Here Vico lays down in explicit detail the pioneer program of a really modern legal science, whose structural pattern will be articulated and brought to harmonious fruition not only by Montesquieu, but by Gustav Hugo, Savigny, Eichhorn, Puchta, i.e., the scholars of Germany's "historical school." [5]

The reasons for Vico's antagonism to Descartes lay in a different conception of man, in a diverging view of the hierarchy and role of man's faculties, in temperamental, environmental, and typological causes. The antithesis Vico-Descartes is, at bottom, the contrast between the mentality of the jurist and that of the mathematician, between the spirit of erudition, and that fostered by the "exact" sciences. As Fontenelle puts it: "Naturally, the genius of mathematical truths and that of profound erudition are opposites: they exclude and despise one another." [6]

Vico's revolt against Descartes has its sources in Descartes himself. Had he not preached independence from authority? Isn't this the meaning of Renato's "universal doubt"?

The exactness and penetration of Vico's analysis of the

[5] Had Friedrich Meinecke (1862–1954), the author of the masterful *Die Entstehung des Historismus* (*The Genesis of Historicism*), known this section of the *De nostri* (and indeed, the *De nostri* itself), he would no doubt have assigned to it the place of honor, in the history of historicism, to which it is entitled.

[6] *Eloge de Bianchini*, in *Œuvres de Fontenelle* (Paris, 1825), II, 232.

major forces permeating the epoch at the close of the seventeenth century are striking. On one side, Gassendism, i.e., Epicureanism, contingency, atomism; on the other, Cartesianism, i.e., the subjectivism of the *cogito,* pan-mathematicism, mechanism. Vico's analysis of the decline of the humanities corresponds point by point to that of Perizonius. Uncanny sagacity is shown by Vico in perceiving that the core of Descartes' system is represented by analytical geometry and by the "clear and distinct perception," ruling out of court any claims of the verisimilar.[7] Having said this, however, distinctions are in order. Vico has no objection to mathematical deductivism when its use is confined to didactic exposition (his *Scienza Nuova seconda* is "entirely built according to the geometric method"); and he does not combat science and the scientific method, but *scientism.* He opposes the encroachments of the mathematical method on nonscientific fields, and underscores the damage resulting from those invasions. He wants a clear demarcation of jurisdictions and competences: the method should be determined by the subject matter, as Aristotle and Pascal had advocated. "That all matters should be managed by the geometrical method, is plainly an exaggeration."

Vico fully shares Descartes' idea of the *unity of science,* in the sense that all individual branches of science are as interacting limbs of a single corpus of knowledge. This idea of the organic interconnection of the sciences is, perhaps, only the counterpart of the pivotal notion of humanism, the *cognatio*

---

[7] Vico's criticism of Descartes' mechanicism ("blind fatality") is of interest to us in the light of modern physics, which has long given up the ideal of pan-mechanism for indeterminacy. An ingenious plea has been made by Lorenzo Giusso (against Croce) for the ascription of Vico to the Baroque age; yet Vico's opposition to pan-mathematicism amounts to a declaration of war against the "central" ideology of the Baroque. See Anneliese Maier, *Die Mechanisierung des Weltbildes* (Leipzig: F. Meiner, 1938), and the solid, important volume of Dijksterhuis, *The Mechanization of the World-Picture* (Oxford: Clarendon Press, 1961). The central ideology of the Baroque is the complete mathematization of all the domains of life and thought.

of all humanistic disciplines, as propounded by Cicero. In the domain of science, it is Descartes who voices it impressively for the first time, in the *Rules*. A corollary of this view of the unity of science is the affirmation that all single sciences benefit by this reciprocity, and progress results. Sketching the state of scientific knowledge of his day, Vico makes an effective polemical point by observing that forward strides in his own and recent times were brought about by that very reciprocity. The unity of knowledge is also postulated at the close of the *De nostri*, where he deplores the anarchy of the teaching methods in the university of his home town, and pleads for unity in the corpus of subject matters. While he is opposed to the tyranny of Descartes's methodological monism, i.e., the application of geometrical procedures to any field lying outside their legitimate sphere, he opposes equally the methodological anarchy prevailing in the teaching of the humanities. *While the* De nostri's *main theme is the deplorability of the extrapolation of method, the work closes with an appeal for the organic unity of culture.*

Descartes left no work specifically dealing with education. But it has frequently been remarked that the *Discourse on Method* does contain a set of principles which are as valid in the domain of pedagogy as they are in the theory of cognition and in scientific research. Accordingly, it has been asserted that Part One of the *Discourse* is a chapter in the history of educational thought. The same claim could be advanced for Part Two, which contains the famous four rules that are to guide the mind in its pursuit of truth. And a great educational value attaches to the fascinatingly personal, experiential tone with which Descartes reports on his quest for intellectual certitude. The "human interest" of the *Discourse* goes a long way toward explaining its pedagogical stimulation outside the narrow confines of an elite of specialists.

In the field of education proper, the effects of the *Discourse* were felt only indirectly in France, in England, in Germany.

Descartes' *Discourse* shares with Bacon's *Advancement* the unusual characteristic of an oblique impact on pedagogy. The work of Comenius (1592–1670) is the point of maximum influence of Bacon's thought in education. Vico's *Autobiography* was directly inspired by that broadly autobiographical essay, Descartes' *Discourse*.

Descartes made no secret of the very low esteem in which he held languages and rhetorical, literary, and historical studies, and, in general, the classical humanities. It is also known that this attitude becomes exacerbated among the most fervent of his continuators and admirers, such as Malebranche, Antoine Arnauld, and Bernard Lamy. "Those who make their principal study that of languages fall into the practice of being attached only to words": this *obiter dictum* should endear Descartes forever to all language teachers (although, as Gabriel Compayré points out, Descartes' attitude may be accounted for and excused in view of the excessive importance attributed, in his youth, to the study of Greek and Latin). He snaps the bond which had traditionally linked eloquence with the study of the classical languages, and with rhetoric. "Those whose reason is most cogent, even though they still speak in low Breton, and have never learned rhetoric," should be awarded the palm of victory in a contest of fine speaking. An ironical smile plays around the philosopher's lips as he refers, with mock reverence, to "the incomparable power and the beauties of eloquence," and lingers on "the refinements and the enrapturing delights of poetry." He frankly declares that he derived no profit whatever from the *litterae humaniores* that were the staple of instruction in the Jesuit college of La Flèche, where he was educated. (Yet they taught him a vigorous, substantial Latin, which he found most useful as a weapon of defense against the furious attacks of his Dutch enemies.) At the inception of his treatise on *The Passions of the Soul* (1649), he emphasizes that what the Ancients have taught in regard to human passions "is so little, and mostly so little worthy of credence, that I have no hope of ever drawing near to the truth unless I forsake the paths that they took." Critics have not failed to notice that Descartes speaks of Aristotle with a disrespect that is really excessive. For instance, in one of the *Replies* he made to the objections brought up against his *Meditations,* he writes: "Since, on this point, it is only on the authority of Aristotle and of his followers that I am objected to, and since I make no mystery of the fact that I trust Aristotle less than my reason, I do not see why I should greatly worry about answering." Apropos of Galileo's refutation of Aristotle, Descartes states: "Galileo is eloquent in refuting Aristotle; but it is not so difficult to do so."

Descartes has an even lower opinion of the crushingly learned philological and antiquarian erudition that flourished in France, the Low Countries, England, and Germany in the seventeenth century. It was an age of scholarly Goliaths like Jacques Godefroid, Casaubon, Saumaise. Think of the colossal Dutch philologians of that period—what names! Meursius, Gronovius I and II, Noodt, Graevius, Daniel and Nicholas Heinsius, Petrus Burmannus I and II, etc. For Descartes, these men, who laid the basis for modern historical criticism, classical philology, diplomatics, paleography, etc., are merely craftsmen without talent: "Their efforts are exclusively directed toward restoring old works, because at bottom, they are incapable of creating new ones." (These words reverberate in Nietzsche's essay on "The Future of Our Educational Institutions.")

And as for *topics,* which Bacon respected, which was the main staple of rhetorical studies, and which the seventeenth-century schools had installed as the queen of the realm of the "probable," Vico felt that Descartes had completely undermined topics with his theory of the clear and distinct perception.[1] To obtain an idea of how Descartes feels about it,

[1] In Aristotle's *Organon,* topics is defined as the procedure whereby one may build conclusions from "probable" statements concerning any problem whatsoever, and whereby, when speaking in public, one may be protected against self-contradiction (see *Topics* I. 1, 100a18). It has been

it is sufficient to read his letter to Voetius. In this little-known letter, which is couched in sinewy Latin (it is really eloquence scornfully spurning eloquence, as veritable eloquence should, according to Pascal), Descartes speaks of topics in so derogatory a tone as to give us a sense of the chasm separating him from Vico. (But we cannot help but imagine how delighted Vico, as a teacher of rhetoric, would have been to observe the consummate, impetuous verbal fervor with which Descartes

rightly remarked that this procedure, enabling one to find the "lines of argument" based on probability apropos of any given subject, is utterly dissimilar from the "eristic" method devised by the Sophists. Topics is concerned with the *loci communes*, i.e., commonplaces, that is, with certain generalities under which may be subsumed the grounds of evidence bearing upon various subjects. In the Aristotelian *Organon*, the *Topics* are the books dealing with the "merely probable" methods of arguing, i.e., with the "hypothetical" or "verisimilar" syllogisms. Faggin (in his article "Topica," in *Enciclopedia Filosofica* [Venice-Rome: Istituto per la Collaborazione Culturale, 1957], Vol. IV, cols. 1270–1271) remarks that "Aristotle has a distinct awareness of the kinship existing between topics and the dialectics of Plato (Plato's dialectics, in fact, starts from premises which are the antithetical counterpart of the 'apodeictic' form of reasoning)."

Faggin lucidly brings out Vico's antagonism to Descartes in regard to topics. "Vico," he states, "opposing the critical method of the Cartesians, affirms that topics (i.e., the theory of the 'invention' of the lines of argument) should precede 'criticism,' i.e., should precede the judgment about the logical truth of the statements advanced." Specifically, Vico's opposition to the Port Royalists' rejection of topics is based on the following passage from the *Port-Royal Logic* (Part III, chap. 17): "One may cite in testimony almost as many persons who have gone through the course of our studies: there is no one who has learned anything from this artificial method of 'finding' proofs. . . . Is there a single individual who may be able truthfully to maintain that, when he was compelled to deal with a subject, he engaged in reflection about the *loci*, and endeavored to find therein the grounds of which he stood in need?" Francis Bacon, instead—and Vico derives signal encouragement and corroboration from Bacon's position in this matter—is a strenuous supporter of topics. Interesting is the recent revaluation of the usefulness of the *loci*, contained in Vieweg's *Topik und Jurisprudenz* (2nd edn.; Munich: J. C. Beck, 1963). But the question of legal topics is, historically and doctrinally, too involved to be more than barely alluded to here.

blasts at Voetius. There is no better confirmation of Vico's favorite theory, that no orator is so eloquent as when he is speaking about himself.)

Among Descartes' admirers there is none whose antihumanistic attitude is so marked as Malebranche. In *La Recherche de la Vérité (The Search After Truth)*, Book Two, Chapter Five, Malebranche contends that it is "useless enough, to those who live at present, to know whether a man called Aristotle ever lived, and whether such a man ever wrote the works which bear his name." Malebranche deplores "the false reverence that men have for the Ancients" and claims that it produces "a great number of very pernicious effects." It has been said that Malebranche would like to erase from the memory of men all traces of traditional knowledge, all vestiges of ancient culture. This radical antihistoricism, which treats the human mind as a *tabula rasa,* results in enthroning logic in the place of honor among curricular disciplines. This tendency is greatly in evidence in the school programs and the educational theory of the *Pères de l'Oratoire,* especially Bernard Lamy (1640–1715), the author of the *Conversations on the Sciences (Entretiens sur les Sciences,* first edition, 1683), one of the prime documents attesting to Cartesian influence in French educational circles at the time. Lamy writes:

> Experience teaches that, God having given to the soul the principles of the sciences and the intelligence wherewith to understand them, it is merely a question of putting this help to a good use, and of paying attention to those primal truths, from which all other truths derive as from their source. It is therefore only a question of regulating what we call the operations of our mind, namely, perceiving, judging, reasoning, arranging our thoughts, our judgments, our reasonings, in fit order. *Therefore it is by a good training in Logic that our studies ought to begin.*[2]

It is this very practice of placing logic at the portal of the

[2] Italics mine. Quoted from the 1706 edn. of the *Entretiens* (Lyon: Jean Certe), p. 37.

educational process that calls forth from Vico one of his two major objections against the study methods of his time. In Vico's critique the target is not Lamy but the *Port-Royal Logic* by Arnauld and Nicole.[3] The content of this *Art de penser* (a "classic" among Jansenist textbooks) is so difficult, abstract, and remote from the *comun senso volgare* that (as Vico phrases it in his *Autobiography*):

> it throws into utter confusion, in our adolescents, those powers of the youthful mind each of which should be regulated and promoted by a systematic study of specific subject matters; as, for instance, memory by the study of languages, imagination by the reading of poets, historians, and orators, and wit by instruction in linear geometry. The intensive training in logic which they receive at the start of the educational process prematurely leads our young men to criticism. There is an inversion of the *natural* course of the mind's development, by which natural course we are led first to learn, then to judge, and finally to reason; whereas, by the current practice, the student is taught the rules of exact judgment before those of right learning. The result is that we raise a youth incapable of expressing himself except in a devastatingly arid and jejune way; a generation of non-doers, who, disliking action, sit up in judgment about all matters.[4]

The antagonism of the defenders of "synthetic," i.e., Euclidian, geometry toward the new "analytical" geometry of Descartes was, in Italy, as the *De nostri* suggests, one important aspect of the debate concerning the Ancients and moderns. The advance of "analytical" ideas was slow; every inch of the ground was contested by men of considerable reputation in the mathematical field: it is enough to mention the name of Guido Grandi (1671–1746). In the Neapolitan milieu in which Vico lived, one of the most tenacious sup-

---

3 See a detailed exposition of its contents in the article "Arnauld, Antoine" in *Dictionnaire des sciences philosophiques,* ed. Franck (Paris, 1852).

4 Vico, *L'Autobiografia, il Carteggio, e le Poesie varie,* eds. F. Nicolini and B. Croce (2nd edn.; Bari: Laterza, 1929), pp. 13–14.

porters of the "synthetic" geometrical procedure was Paolo
Mattia Doria (1662–1746), to whom Vico's *De Antiquissima*
is inscribed. But reluctance to accept the Cartesian revolution
represented by analytical geometry had manifested itself in
France also, where Pascal and Desargues had been partisans
of the *géometrie synthétique*.[5] It is true that the discovery of
analytical geometry forced synthetic geometry to lie in abey-
ance until the time when the contributions of Lagrange,
Monge, and others, and the development of projective geometry, effected a vigorous resumption of the "synthetic" trend;
but our knowledge of geometrical anti-Cartesianism in the
seventeenth and eighteenth centuries is still too scanty to enable us to discern with precise clarity the varying phases of
that debate. (It is true that the excellent *History of Analytical
Geometry* by Professor Boyer informs us about the positive
aspects of the subject: what we lack is a more circumstantial
account of the opposition to the validity of "analytical"
procedures.)

In the retrospect of time, it is easy to perceive that Vico
hardly understood the complex intellectual itinerary that led
to Descartes' invention of analytical geometry, or the peculiar
character of the mental operations involved in the application
of it. This, I think, is obvious from Vico's remark that it was
the genius of the French language (its so subtle, penetrating,
abstract, intellectualistic cast) that was largely responsible
for the invention of analytical geometry. As a matter of fact,
that invention (as all beginners in the history of mathematics
are aware) was the outcome of an intra-mathematical process,
distinguished by a notable consistence and continuity, and
predicated upon the progress of algebra since the Italian alge-
brists of the *Cinquecento* (Tartaglia, Cardano, Bombelli) leading through Viète to the almost simultaneous discovery of the
new *mathesis* by Fermat and Descartes (Fermat never published the results of his researches). In that inner progress of

[5] See P. Boutroux, "La conception, synthétiste des mathématiques,"
chap. 2 in *L'idéal scientifique des mathématiciens* (Paris: F. Alcan, 1920),
pp. 80–130.

mathematical thought, the role of Viète was central (especially in the algorithmic, notational field), and Descartes himself declared that he took up exactly where Viète had left off. The charge that Vico had but a hazy notion of the specific operations implied in the application of the Cartesian "analysis" receives strong support from the comparison he uses, in the *De nostri,* to describe the process of equation-solving. He likens it to the corybantic soul-state of the god-haunted, prophetic Sybil, the priestess, trying to shake off from her body the "possession" of the divine frenzy. This image, besides contradicting the accusation of abstract intellectualism, which runs like a red thread throughout Vico's critique of Descartes, thoroughly misrepresents the operations of algebra which, obviously, have nothing in common with "Dionysiac" fury.[6]

[6] After having remarked that to consider the work of Descartes simply as the systematization, and, so to speak, as the codification of previous discoveries, constitutes a complete misunderstanding, Jacques Chevalier determines the originality of Descartes' achievement as follows: "All the materials of the new science [analytical geometry] were ready prior to him. Geometrical analysis had been set up by Apollonius, apropos of the study of conical sections; algebraic analysis had been elaborated by Viète; Fermat, in his *Isagoge ad locos planos et solidos,* had described with perfect clarity the equation of a *locus.* Even the use of the rectangular co-ordinates had been introduced, as early as the 14th century, by Nicholas Oresme, and, under the name of *longitudines* (abscisses) and *latitudines* (ordinates) had been currently taught in medieval schools. The particular achievement of Descartes was that he tackled the question from its general aspect . . . as an expression of a panoptic view over science and the human mind. Thanks to this view, he was able to perceive the correlation of all specialized disciplines, and to make them converge to a single end. Descartes' predecessors, Apollonius, Oresme, Fermat, had given him examples of the application of this method: but these examples remained in the status of [disconnected] procedures, by reason of the lack of a general conception and of rational co-ordination. The Greek 'analysts,' for instance, were compelled to establish 'a separate theorem for each particular case.' Descartes, instead, with a single leap forward leaves behind the Ancients and Fermat himself: he *sees why* the procedures of the calculus are successful in the particular cases, and this *why* is the recognition of a grand method, simple and general, applicable to all cases, irrespective of the nature of the case considered. Before him, metrical relationships were only a section of geometry. Descartes perceives that all geometry may

But more important than this misunderstanding of algebra is the essential fact that Vico understood that Descartes had performed a real revolution in men's thinking by his procedure of rendering the geometrical abstract, or, to be more precise, by his de-figurization of the geometrical, and by its conversion into algebraic values. We have seen that Vico perfectly grasped the idea of the unity of science and of the interplay of various branches of science, which characterizes the Cartesian system. Descartes' second great contribution, i.e., the establishment of the equivalence of the algebraic with the geometrical expression of the same quantity (Descartes indicates this equivalence by writing the equation of the circle and by devising the "Cartesian" co-ordinates) was, likewise, fully grasped by the Neapolitan philosopher (aided perhaps by his friend Paolo Mattia Doria). Vico perceived that that process of abstraction was the authentic symbol of the onward march of science. As Louis Mesnard observes, it was Descartes' *Geometry,* published in the same year (1637) as the *Discourse,* that opened the era of modern mathematics by rendering the discoveries of Leibniz and Newton possible.[7] What Vico, and, for that matter, none but an unusually sharp-sighted soothsayer in post-Cartesian times, could have anticipated is that as mathematical thought progressively developed, the impact of the new algebra on geometry would lead to new discoveries in the field of geometry itself.

A few words must be added regarding Vico's contraposition of synthetic geometry to Cartesian *ars analytica.* By insisting on that contraposition, he seized on a point of great importance in the philosophy of mathematics. A great debate went on for instance, in the second and third decade of our century, between the partisans of the intuitionalistic and the logistic con-

---

be metrical, and that, on becoming metrical, it becomes analytical; not only that, he affirms moreover that there is no geometry but a metrical one. *That* constitutes his great discovery. . . ." Jacques Chevalier, *Descartes,* pp. 126–127.

7 Descartes, *Discours de la méthode, texte et commentaire en regard,* ed. L. Mesnard (Paris, n.d.), p. 62.

ception of the foundations of mathematics, as attested by such outstanding works as H. Weyl's *Philosophy of Mathematics and the Sciences of Nature* (1927), and A. Heyting's *The Quest for the Basis of Mathematics, Intuitionalism and Theory of Demonstration* (1934). The basic antithesis between intuitionalism and logicism affects not only pure logic and mathematics, but the whole of science, insofar as science represents a rational experience. To have realized the significance of such an antithesis constitutes no small claim to fame in the history of ideas.

Vico believes in the existence of a *psychogenetic law*, by which the individual develops through a certain series of phases, the sequential order of which is immutably fixed by nature. These stages parallel an equally immutable set of "culture stages" which the whole of mankind has traversed in its growth from infancy to adulthood, from primitivism to civilization. In other words, the single individual recapitulates the entire process of development of the species. Vico believes that education should be founded on this "natural order of stages," i.e., he pleads that education should "conform" with nature.

The presence of this idea in the *De nostri* is interesting for several reasons, only two of which will receive attention here. First, it reveals Vico's links with the Baroque age (but, as mentioned, he is in reaction to its "central ideology," the complete mathematization of all life and thought); second, it makes him the direct precursor of Jean-Jacques Rousseau, whose *Émile,* as we all know, is based on the concept of *éducation naturelle.* In regard to the first point, it is true that the two most prominent pedagogic thinkers of the Baroque age, Ratke and Comenius, had already propounded that concept. But in Ratke and Comenius, that theme remains confined to the domain of education. Vico, instead, extends the idea beyond education to constitute the core of a full-fledged philosophical vision of history, which comes to complete blossoming in the *Scienza Nuova.* In regard to the second point, there are several aspects in which Vico distinctly anticipates Rousseau, and which have been ably studied by Italian critics. They have emphasized, as features common to both thinkers, the self-creativeness of human nature (a concept that had such appeal for Michelet that he made it the pivot of his interpretation of the history of France); the defense of the child's world against the oppression of the adult; the conscious certitude that the positive results of any educational method are dependent upon the recognition of the functional autonomy of childhood; the thesis of the predominantly nonrational nature of the child; the incongruity of a type of education that proposes the turning out of "erudite adolescents and senile children." Professor Remo Fornaca spells out the dissimilarities between the *De nostri* and the *Émile,* and, although affirming Vico's role as a pioneer of this view, finds that the advantages of Rousseau's educational views lie in the greater depth of his psychology of

> . . . the evolutional age, in a more appropriate realism of educational method, in the quest for a meeting-point between the child and the outward world, in Rousseau's precise determination of the function and limits of the action of the teacher, in the different evaluation of culture and of its relationships with the evolution of mankind, in the different choice and arrangement of the subject matters, and finally, in the aim which Rousseau assigns to education.[1]

It is one of the major contributions of the *De nostri* to have strongly underlined the fact that education must be based on psychology, and to have pointed out the specific, non-interchangeable, "non-fungible" character of each of the stages of growth of the human mind. The unique quality of the child's reaction to reality is, consequently, highlighted. By this recog-

[1] Remo Fornaca, *Il pensiero educativo di Giambattista Vico* (Torino: Giappichelli, 1957), p. 209; an excellent monograph on Vico's educational thought. An accurate determination of the historical relationship between the two thinkers is to be found in F. Nicolini's study, *Vico e Rousseau* (Naples: Giannini, 1949; first published in "Atti dell Accademia Pontaniana," N.S. I, 1947–1948).

nition of the uniqueness of the child's psychology, Vico deserves to be saluted as the authentic precursor of Rousseau. He also proves himself to be the starter of that revolution (which is manifested also in the Cartesian turn from objective realism to the subjectivism of the *cogito*, and in the Kantian *Wendung* of the *Critique of Pure Reason*) by which attention shifts from educator to pupil, from formalism in curricular content to modes of apperception and living assimilation. Vico is the true forerunner of educational, and especially child-educational, psychology. The delimitation of child psychology as an autonomous field of investigation comes after Vico's time; its "germinal" epoch was the second half of the eighteenth century, the names to remember being Rousseau, Tiedemann, Wetzel, Tetens, Trapp, Heusinger. The earliest systematic treatment was that by W. T. Preyer, in *Die Seele des Kindes,* which appeared in 1882.[2] It was as late as the second half of the nineteenth century (and in this lateness the slow permeation of European thought by the ideas of Rousseau is perceptible) that general acceptance was accorded the view that the child is not "a small adult in infantile form," but a human being endowed with its own values, its own world of sensations, perceptions, and feelings, its own peculiar way of intuiting reality. This trend Vico visibly anticipates. Misleading as may be the view that Vico was an outright pre-Romanticist, there is a whole aspect of the German Romantic movement of which he seems to have been the ancestor (via Herder, perhaps): that aspect which stresses poetical imagination, the fairy tale, the "primitive," the creative unconscious. It is with this aspect that Vico's revaluation and rehabilitation of the *phantasia puerilis* over against the Cartesian dogmatization of *intellectus purus* is connected.

An important feature in the *De nostri* is the *verum ipsum factum*—"knowledge is equipollent to operation"—the epistemologic criterion consciously set up in opposition to the

[2] English translation by H. W. Brown, *The Mind of the Child* (New York: D. Appleton and Company, 1888–1889).

Cartesian standard of the clear and distinct perception. Croce calls the aggregate of ideas contained in the *verum ipsum factum* the initial form of Vico's theory of cognition. According to Vico, we have true knowledge when the thinking and the doing are performed by the identical person. Man, who is the maker of his own history, can "cognize" it: knowledge is tantamount to operation. We shall not go into the many corollaries that spring from that formula,[1] but are here interested only in the implications it has for educational theory. Its significance is nothing less than *axial*. That formula, besides being the central hinge of historicism, sets up the principle, extremely important for pedagogy, of the "constructive" character of true knowledge. Professor Aliotta, whose exposition of Vico's educational thought is distinguished by a sagacious clarity, after pointing out that a shortcoming of the Cartesian method is the theory of innate ideas (by which the human spirit finds within itself truths that God has implanted), notes the acumen of Vico's remark that the fact of our finding in ourselves an idea, however clear and evident, does not constitute true knowledge. That idea, Aliotta says, may be something *passively* accepted, something like a gift that is being received, and that remains in our spirit like an extraneous entity. Instead, we gain full understanding of an idea when we achieve a thorough appropriation of it, when we have "made it ourselves." [2] Vico is persuaded that the certitude of geometrical truths is based exactly on this principle. (The "constructive" character of geometrical truths had already been perceived by Hobbes. In the opening section of his *De corpore*, he states that *geometrica demonstramus quia facimus*: geometry is our own creation, our own production;

---

[1] For the field of history, they have been set forth with admirable lucidity by U. Redano, article "Il pensiero storiografico dal Rinascimento all'Illuminismo," in *Questioni di storia moderna* (Milan: Marzorati), pp. 885–901; and by Collingwood, *The Idea of History* (2nd edn.; Oxford: Oxford University Press, 1951).

[2] A. Aliotta, *Disegno storico della pedagogia* (Naples: Perrella, 1951), pp. 222–223.

hence, we have full knowledge of it.) Vico draws the consequence that, since the physical world has not been created by
us, but by God, it is God alone who has thorough knowledge
of it. Aliotta continues:

> In the pedagogical field, Vico's principle *verum ipsum
> factum* has proved to be extremely fertile. In the "active
> school," for instance, the learner must not find truth ei-
> ther outside himself, adopting it passively (a process
> which can be likened to pouring a liquid through a fun-
> nel into a container), nor must he find it in himself by
> accepting it as an initial datum, as a gift, without con-
> tributing anything of his own. The learner, instead,
> should take an active role, a dynamic initiative, in the
> construction of knowledge. Only thus will he be able to
> attain a true possession of it.

Vico attaches signal importance to "effort," to personal par-
ticipation, to individual initiative, in the assimilation, one
may say "sanguification" (transformation into *succum et san-
guinem*) of what Sir Philip Sidney would call "the sweet food
of academic institution" (*institutio:* the Latin word for instruction). There could be no more explicit rejection of the
adjustment theory of behaviorism; no more outspoken support, with two centuries of anticipation, of John Dewey's conception of the dynamic process of learning.

In his reply to Article Ten of Volume Eight of the *Gior-
nale dei Letterati d'Italia* (Venice, 1711), Vico writes:

> Do you wish to teach me a scientific truth? Assign to me
> the reason that is entirely contained within me, so that
> I may understand in my way a term, may establish a re-
> lationship that I institute between two or more abstract
> ideas; ideas which, as a consequence, are contained within
> me. Let us start from a feigned indivisible, let us stop at
> an imagined infinite, and you will be able to tell me,
> "Give me a demonstration of the theorem that has been
> proposed," which is equivalent to saying: Create the truth
> that you wish to cognize; and I, in cognizing the truth that
> you have proposed to me, will "make" it in such a way
> that there will be no possibility of my doubting it, since I
> am the very one who has produced it.

There is no more forceful and lapidary expression of the *verum ipsum factum*.[3]

In closing, we should re-emphasize the value that the *De nostri* has as the "defense and illustration" (as Du Bellay would phrase it) of a modern humanism, which aims at fruitful coexistence of the sciences and the *humaniora*. Maria Goretti, in the final section of the Introduction to her own edition of the *De nostri*, formulates her conclusion in noble words which we are pleased to insert here. Taking up the idea, which we share, that Vico is not really in polemics against Descartes, but against the degenerations and dogmatizations of Cartesianism, as exemplified by Malebranche, Lamy, Arnauld, etc., she declares that

> Thus Vico, the opponent of the geometric spirit, who is not, however, deaf to the powerful voices of the modern achievements of science and technic, appears to us, not so much the adversary of the Cartesian spirit, as, rather, the enemy of the intellectualistic schema: a schema which forces tumultuous, contradictory human nature into the straightjacket of an absolute truth, of a truth excogitated, dreamt of, but never to be actually met with in reality.

And she sums up Vico's significance in the history of the idea of humanism as follows:

> On the other hand, he, the eulogizer of eloquence, the estimator of that verisimilitude [4] which makes up the

3 Vico, *Le Orazione Inaugurali, il De Italorum sapientia, e le Polemiche,* eds. G. Gentile and F. Nicolini (Bari: Laterza, 1914), p. 258. The key passages of Vico's work bearing on the *verum ipsum factum* are found in *De Antiquissima,* ed. Fausto Nicolini (Bari: Laterza, 1914), chap. 1, p. 62, chap. 3, p. 76; *Principi d'una Scienza Nuova,* Book I, sec. 2; and *Degli elementi,* § 14.

4 That is, the revaluator of those *probabiles tantum cognitiones* which Descartes discards in Rule II of the *Rules for the Direction of the Mind,* where we read: "Per hanc propositionem rejicimus omnes probabiles tantum cognitiones, nec nisi perfecte cogniti, et de quibus dubitari non potest, statuimus esse credendum." ("By this proposition we reject all merely probable ideas, and set down that no belief should be accorded except to those which are perfectly known, and which allow of no doubt.")

warp and woof of vital human communication, appears to us not only as the bold asserter of human freedom in a universe dominated by Descartes, not only as the vindicator of "worldly" reality, but also as the master of modern humanism. Vico precisely establishes humanism's most authentic and durable values. These values are not to be found in traditional conservatism (against which the charges of immobilism, of formalism, are thoroughly justified) but are expressed by the emphasis which he lays on the reality of man. This reality is unitary and complex, made up not only of intelligence, but of passion and sensuousness as well. And therefore, if human dignity consists in the conquest of spiritual values, this conquest is also the transfiguration of the turbid passionality which stirs and boils in human hearts; consequently, the school, and science, if they wish to be human, i.e., if they wish to be instruments of education, tools for shaping the minds of our young men, should also address themselves to their hearts; in enlightening their intellects, they should also kindle their wills and spark their enthusiasm.[5]

It is hoped that through the present appearance in English of Vico's *De nostri,* the forces which are presently at work in the great Anglo-Saxon community, building the bases of a new, modern humanism, nourished by the past but looking forward to the future, will receive stimulation, direction, and inspiration.

---

[5] Introduction to Vico, *De nostri,* ed. Maria Goretti (Lemonnier: Florence, 1958), pp. 20-21.

CHRONOLOGY OF VICO'S PRINCIPAL WRITINGS

Inaugural Orations 1699–1707

De nostri temporis studiorum ratione 1709
(On the Study Methods of Our Time)

De antiquissima Italorum sapientia 1710
(On the Most Ancient Wisdom of the Italians)

Institutiones oratoriae 1711 and 1738 editions
(Course Manual on Institutes of Oratory)

Il diritto universale 1720–22
(Universal Law)

> *De uno universi iuris principio et fine uno* 1720
> (On the One Principle and the One End of Universal Law)

> *De constantia iurisprudentis* 1721
> (On the Constancy of the Jurisprudent)

> *Notae in duos libros* 1722
> (Notes on the above two works)

Scienza nuova 1725
(First New Science)

Vita di Giambattista Vico scritta da se medesimo 1725–28
(Autobiography)

Vici vindiciae: Notae in "Acta Eruditorum" Lipsiensia 1729
   (Reply to the Leipzig review of the First New Science)

Scienza nuova seconda 1730–1744
   (New Science)

Supplement to the Autobiography 1731

De mente heroica 1732
   (On the Heroic Mind)

Le accademie e i rapporti tra la filosofia e l'eloquenza 1737
   (The Academies and the Relation between Philosophy and
   Eloquence)

NOTE ON THE TEXT

The original Latin text of the *De nostri* from which this translation was made is that contained in Volume I, *Orazioni Inaugurali,* pages 76–121, of Vico's *Opere,* edited by Fausto Nicolini and B. Croce (8 vols.; Bari: Laterza, 1914–1941). The present paragraph separations have been made by the translator, as have also the section divisions. The Table of Contents is a translation of Vico's own summary of the *De nostri.*

ON THE
STUDY METHODS
OF OUR TIME

I

In his small but priceless treatise entitled *De dignitate et de augmentis scientiarum*,[1] Francis Bacon undertakes to point

[1] (*Of the Dignity and Advancement of Learning*.) Bacon's project was of a striking, almost superhuman grandeur. He envisaged nothing less than the total reconstruction of the fabric of science: *Instauratio magna* (*The Great Instauration*). He was keenly conscious of the gigantic dimensions of his plan, for the realization of which he foresaw that a limited time would be utterly insufficient. "And certainly," he writes, "it may be objected to me with truth that my words require an age, a whole age, perhaps, to prove them, and many ages to perfect them."

The *De dignitate* was published in 1623, as an expansion of the *Two Books of Proficience and Advancement of Learning* which appeared in 1603–1605. It was meant to be Part I of the *Instauratio magna*. Part II is the *Novum organum* (*The New Organon*), i.e., the instrument to be substituted for the Ancients' superficial induction and the syllogistic method.

In order to achieve the reconstruction of science, as G. Fonsegrive points out, it was necessary, first, to dismantle traditional science (this was performed in the *De dignitate*); secondly, to establish the method by which true science can be attained (this was done in the *Novum organum*); finally, to construct modern science, and this would have been accomplished in the last part of the *Instauratio* which was left unfinished.

The general plan of the *Instauratio magna* was sketched (1620) in the Introduction of the *Novum organum*. An outline of Part I of *Instauratio* appears in the *Two Books of Proficience and Advancement of Learning* of 1603–1605.

In the *De dignitate*, after having defended science from the objections of theologians and writers on politics, Bacon extols its value (*dignitas*), and examines, one by one, the various branches of knowledge. What new sciences should be added to those already existing are listed in the prospectus of *desiderata* ("The New World of Sciences") affixed as an Appendix to this work. Among these new sciences are the history of culture, philosophical grammar, a treatise on the common principles (axioms) of the sciences, comparative anatomy, literary history, history of the arts, philosophy of law, etc.

The plan of the *Instauratio magna* called for six parts, as follows. Part I: a systematic division of all sciences, and a radical revision of their present status. Part II: explanation of principles which should guide

3

out what new arts and sciences should be added to those we already possess, and suggests how we may enlarge our stock of knowledge, [as far as necessary,] so that human wisdom may be brought to complete perfection.

But, while he discovers a new cosmos of sciences, the great Chancellor proves to be rather the pioneer of a completely new universe than a prospector of this world of ours. His vast demands so exceed the utmost extent of man's effort that he seems to have indicated how we fall short of achieving an absolutely complete system of sciences rather than how we may remedy our cultural gaps.

This was so, I believe, because those who occupy the heights of power yearn for the immense and the infinite. Thus Bacon acted in the intellectual field like the potentates of mighty empires, who, having gained supremacy in human affairs, squander immense wealth in attempts against the order of Nature herself, by paving the seas with stones, mastering mountains with sail, and other vain exploits forbidden by nature.

No doubt all that man is given to know is, like man himself, limited and imperfect. Therefore, if we compare our times with those of the Ancients—if we weigh, on both sides, the advantages and deficiencies of learning—our achievements and those of Antiquity would, by and large, balance.

We, the men of the modern age, have discovered many things of which the Ancients were entirely ignorant; the Ancients, on the other hand, knew much still unknown to us.

---

our investigation and interpretation of nature, that is, an exposition of the new method. Part III: natural and experimental history destined for the establishment of philosophy, i.e., collection of the empirical materials to which the new method is to be applied. Part IV: "the ladder of the Intellect," showing the twofold use, inductive and deductive, of the human mind in the search for laws. Part V: anticipation of truth, i.e., the discoveries realized by the traditional method. Part VI: definite systematization of operational science.

As we stated, only Part I (*De dignitate*) and Part II (*Novum organum*) were composed; Part III is present in the form of a heterogeneous assemblage of scientific materials, *Sylva sylvarum* (*Forest of Materials*).

We enjoy many techniques which enable us to make progress in some branch of intellectual or practical activity; they likewise had talents for progress in other fields. They devoted all their activity to certain arts which we almost totally neglect; we pursue some others which they apparently scorned. Many disciplines conveniently unified by the Ancients have been partitioned by us; a certain number which they inconveniently kept separate, we treat as unified. Finally, not a few sectors of culture have changed both appearance and name.

The foregoing provides the theme of the present discourse: Which study method is finer and better, ours or the Ancients'? In developing this topic I shall illustrate by examples the advantages and drawbacks of the respective methods. I shall specify which of the drawbacks of our procedures may be avoided, and how; and whether those which cannot be eliminated have their counterparts in particular shortcomings by which the Ancients were handicapped.

Unless I am mistaken, this theme is new; but the knowledge of it is so important, that I am amazed it has not been treated yet. In the hope of escaping censure, I ask you to give thought to the fact that my purpose is not to criticize the drawbacks of the study methods of our age or of those of antiquity, but rather to compare the advantages afforded by the study methods of the two epochs.

This matter is of direct concern to you: even if you know more than the Ancients in some fields, you should not accept knowing less in others. You should make use of a method by which you can acquire, on the whole, more knowledge than the Ancients, and, being aware of the shortcomings of ancient methods of study, you may endure the unavoidable inconveniences of our own.

The better to grasp the subject I am proposing to you, you should distinctly realize that in the present discourse I do not intend to draw parallels between individual branches of knowledge, single fields of sciences or arts of ancient and modern times.

My goal, instead, is to indicate in what respect our study methods are superior to those of the Ancients; to discover in what they are inferior, and how we may remedy this inferiority.

For our purpose we must, if not separate, at least set up a distinction between new arts, sciences, and inventions on one hand, and new *instruments* and aids to knowledge on the other. The former are the constituent material of learning; the latter are the way and the means, precisely the subject of our discourse.

Every study method may be said to be made up of three things: instruments, complementary aids, and the aim envisaged. The instruments presuppose and include a systematic, orderly manner of proceeding; the apprentice who, after suitable training, undertakes the task of mastering a certain art or science, should approach it in an appropriate and well-ordered fashion. Instruments are antecedent to the task of learning; complementary aids and procedures are concomitant with that task. As for the aim envisaged, although its attainment is subsequent to the process of learning, it should never be lost sight of by the learner, neither at the beginning nor during the entire learning process.

We shall arrange our discourse in corresponding order, and discuss first the instruments, then the aids to our method of study. As for the aim, it should circulate, like a blood-stream, through the entire body of the learning process. Consequently, just as the blood's pulsation may best be studied at the spot where the arterial beat is most perceptible, so the aim of our study methods shall be treated at the point where it assumes the greatest prominence.

Some of the new instruments of science are, themselves, sciences; others are arts; still others, products of either art or nature. Modern philosophical "critique" is the common instrument of all our sciences and arts.[2] The instrument of

---

[2] Vico's reference is to the Cartesian method, the Cartesian "revolution of logic," in the famous four rules of the *Discourse on Method*. Method

is defined by Descartes as "a set of certain and easy rules, such that any-
one, who obeys them exactly, will, first, never take anything false for
true, and secondly, will advance step by step, without waste of mental effort, until he has achieved the knowledge of everything which does
not surpass his capacity of understanding" (*Rules for the Direction of
the Mind*, Rule 4). In order to grasp the full, epochal significance of
the Cartesian method, a study not only of the *Discourse* but also of the
Rules is indispensable. It is furthermore necessary to keep in mind the
specific features which distinguish the Cartesian from the Scholastic, syllogistic method. Descartes rejects "the Scholastic logic based on compre-
hension and connotation" (L. J. Beck, *The Method of Descartes: A Study
of the Regulae* [Oxford: Clarendon Press, 1952], p. 106). As is well known,
Descartes' method is based on the procedures of mathematics. "He attacks
the idea of a science of method which assumes . . . that it can give rules
and precepts for reasoning which are independent altogether of the nature
of the content about which the reasoning occurs" (Beck, p. 105), that is,
rules and precepts which are purely formal (*syllogismorum formae*).
Aliquié points out that the Cartesian inference, being of the mathematical
type, is utterly unlike the syllogism, "which operates by telescoping concepts different in extent and scope" (F. Alquié, *Descartes, l'homme et
l'oeuvre* [Paris: Hatier-Boivin, 1956], p. 32). In Descartes, the relationship which is at the basis of reasoning is not one of inherence.
It is, most often, a relationship between quantities, which enables us to
fix the place of such quantities within a certain "order" (Alquié). Most
enlightening, for the purpose of understanding the character, nature, and
scope of the Cartesian method, is an attentive examination of the *Geometry*,
the *Dioptrics* and the *Meteorology*, where the Cartesian method may be
seen in action, and where its function as a logic of scientific discovery
can be observed at close range. The Cartesian method was amply elaborated (also in regard to the "moral" sciences) in the *Port-Royal Logic*
(1662) by A. Arnauld and Pierre Nicole (Pascal is said to have contributed
to the second edition of this book); and in Book VI of the *Recherche de
la Vérité* (*The Search After Truth*) by Malebranche. A signally important
variation of the Cartesian method is Spinoza's *Tractatus de intellectus
emendatione* (*Treatise on the Improvement of the Understanding*). It
has been remarked that, although Leibniz was mainly engaged in carrying
out a reconciliation of the Aristotelian-Scholastic with the Cartesian
method on the basis of the reciprocal relations of analysis and synthesis,
he, notwithstanding his objections against Descartes, may be viewed as a
continuator of the Cartesian method. It was this method which enabled
him to develop universal mathematics *qua* logistics (mathematical logic)
and logical calculus, under the name of *ars combinatoria*. (See S. Cara-
mella, article "Metodo," in *Enciclopedia Filosofica* [Venice-Rome: Istituto
per la Collaborazione Culturale, 1957], III, cols. 562–573.)

geometry is "analysis"; [3] that of physics, geometry, plus the geometrical method (and, in a certain sense, modern mechanics). The instrument of medicine is chemistry and its offshoot, pharmacological chemistry. The instrument of anatomy is the microscope; that of astronomy, the telescope; that of geography, the mariner's needle.

As for "complementary aids," I include among them the orderly reduction to systematic rules, of a number of subjects which the Ancients were wont to entrust to practical common sense. Complementary aids are also works of literature and of the fine arts whose excellence designates them as patterns of perfection; the types used in the printing; and universities as institutions of learning.

In view of the easy accessibility, usefulness and value of the

---

[3] Vico used the word "analysis" in two senses. The first is that of mathematical analysis (in geometry, the adjective "analytic" has come to mean "using algebraic methods"). It is important to distinguish the meaning that Vico attaches to "analysis" (a meaning identical to that assigned to it by Descartes) from the modern meaning, in which "analysis" is equivalent to "calculus." (Analytical geometry is the background for the calculus, invented by Newton and Leibniz.) Analysis is the first step of the Cartesian method. Rule 5 of the *Rules For the Direction of the Mind*, embodying the second and third Rule of the *Discourse*, asserts that "the exact observance of the method will be secured if (*a*) we reduce involved and obscure propositions, step by step, to more simple ones; and if then (*b*) we start from our intellectual intuition into the simplest propositions, and endeavor, by retracing our path through the same steps, to work out our way up to the knowledge of all the others." Descartes' method is the analytico-synthetic: in L. J. Beck's words, "every complex must be resolved by analysis into simple constituents or parts, and then, by the inverse process, synthesized, by combining those constituents in such an order that their interrelations or connexions, when they are combined together, are manifestly intelligible" (*The Method of Descartes*, pp. 278–279).

The second sense in which Vico uses the word "analysis" (in this passage of the *De nostri*, both senses are present) is that of "analytical geometry," a discipline, if not invented, triumphantly illustrated and applied by Descartes, and which, by a combination of algebra (*ars analytica*) and geometry, resulted in a method so powerful that, thanks to it, geometry made more progress in half a century than in the fifteen preceding centuries.

complementary aids, our study methods seem, beyond any doubt, to be better and more correct than those of the Ancients, whether in regard to facility, or to utility, or to merit.

As for the aim of all kinds of intellectual pursuits: one only is kept in view, one is pursued, one is honored by all: Truth.

II

Modern philosophical critique supplies us with a fundamental verity of which we can be certain even when assailed by doubt. That critique could rout the skepticism even of the New Academy.[4]

In addition, "analysis" (i.e., analytical geometry) empowers us to puzzle out with astonishing ease geometrical problems which the Ancients found impossible to solve.

Like us, the Ancients utilized geometry and mechanics as instruments of research in physics, but not as a constant practice. We apply them consistently, and in better form.

Let us leave aside the question whether geometry has undergone greater development by means of *"analysis,"* and whether modern mechanics constitutes something new. What cannot be denied is the fact that leading investigators have available to them a science enriched by a number of new and extremely ingenious discoveries. Modern scientists, seeking for guidance in their exploration of the dark pathways of nature, have introduced the geometrical method into physics. Holding to this

---

4 The New Academy is the Second Platonic Academy (or School), whose major representatives were Arcesilaus (*ca.* 315–240 B.C.) and Carneades (*ca.* 214–129 B.C.), and which was marked by a radical epistemological skepticism (in contrast to the First and Third Platonic Academy, characterized by a predominantly dogmatic orientation of thought). Vico's allusion is to the Cartesian *cogito,* by which the certainty of existence is to be found in the depths of the doubting consciousness itself; be it noted that Vico did not believe that Descartes had put to flight, had "routed" skepticism; he demonstrates the contrary in his *De antiquissima Italiorum sapientia (On the Very Ancient Wisdom of the Italians,* which is a prosecution and expansion of the anti-Cartesian polemic broached in the *De nostri).*

method as to Ariadne's thread, they can reach the end of their appointed journey. Do not consider them as groping practitioners of physics: they are to be viewed, instead, as the grand architects of this limitless fabric of the world: able to give a detailed account of the ensemble of principles according to which God has built this admirable structure of the cosmos.

Chemistry, of which the Ancients were totally ignorant, has made outstanding contributions to medicine. Having observed the similarity which exists between the various phenomena of the human body and those of chemistry, the healing art has been able, not only to hazard guesses concerning many physiological functions and disorders, but to make these plainly discernible to the human eye.

Pharmacology, of course, a derivate of chemistry, was among the ancients merely a desideratum. Nowadays, we have converted that desideratum into a reality. Some of our researchers have applied chemistry to physics; others, mechanics to medicine. Our physical chemistry can faithfully, and, so to speak, *manually*, reproduce a number of meteors and other physical phenomena. Mechanical medicine can describe, by inferences drawn from the motions of machines, the diseases of the human body, and can treat them successfully. And anatomy clearly reveals not only the circulation of the blood, but the nerve-roots, countless humors, vessels and ducts of the human body (notice that such descriptions already constitute notable advances over ancient medicine), and moreover—thanks to the microscope—the nature of miliary glands, of the most minute internal organs, of plants, of silkworms, and of insects. To modern anatomy, furthermore, we are indebted for an insight into the process of generation, as demonstrated by the growth of the incubated egg. All these things were entirely outside of the narrow range of sight of the science of the Ancients; modern science throws a flood of light upon them.

As for astronomy, the modern telescope has brought within our ken a multitude of new stars, the variability of sun-spots, and phases of the planets. These discoveries have made us aware of several defects in the cosmological system of Ptolemy.[5]

In the domain of geographical exploration, the Ancients guessed vaguely, in a prophetic sort of way, at the existence of transoceanic lands. By the use of the mariner's compass, the modern age has actually discovered them. As a result, a wonderful luster has been bestowed upon geography.

It seems almost unbelievable that in our days men should not only be able to circumnavigate the globe along with the sun, but to outreach the sun's march and to negotiate its full course in less time than it takes that planet to complete it.[6]

From geometry and physics, taught by the present method, the science of mechanics has received major impulses and has rendered possible a great number of outstanding and marvelous inventions, which have vastly enriched human society. It may be said that it is from these three sciences that our technique of warfare derives. Our art of war is so immeasurably superior to that of the Ancients, that, compared with our technique of fortifying and attacking cities, Minerva would contemn her own Athenian citadel and Jupiter would scorn his three-pronged lightning as a blunt and cumbersome weapon.

Such are the "instruments" employed by our modern sciences; let us now turn to the complementary aids employed in the various sectors of our culture.

Systematic treatments (*artes*) have been set up of certain

[5] Claudius Ptolemaeus (*ca.* A.D. 100–170), the most celebrated astronomer and geographer of antiquity, author of the *Almagest* (13 books) in which he develops the theory that the earth is stationary, with the sun, moon, and other planets revolving around it. This theory dominated scientific research in celestial phenomena for about 1400 years, until Copernicus.

[6] Vico means that in his epoch a voyage of circumnavigation could be performed in a lesser time than it takes the sun to revolve around the earth (four seasons). This does not mean that Vico did not believe in the heliocentric system: he speaks from the viewpoint of the Ancients, for whom geocentrism was the accepted dogma (in spite of Aristarchus of Samos, *ca.* 320–250 B.C., whose heliocentrism theory Copernicus had to rediscover).

subjects which the Ancients left to unaided common sense. Among these subjects is the law, which the Ancients, balked by the difficulty of the task, gave up hope of organizing into a systematically arranged, methodical body of theory.

In the fields of poetry, oratory, painting, sculpture, and other fine arts, based on the imitation of nature, we possess a wealth of supremely accomplished productions, on which the admiration of posterity has conferred the prestige of arche-typal exemplarity. Thanks to the guidance offered by these masterworks, we are able to imitate, correctly and easily, Na-ture at her best. The invention of printing places at our dis-posal an enormous number of books. Hence, our scholars are not compelled to restrict their competence to the knowledge of one or another author, but can master a multiple, diversi-fied, almost boundless domain of culture.

Finally, we have great institutions of learning, i.e., univer-sities, which are the repositories of all our sciences and arts, and where the intellectual, spiritual, and linguistic abilities of men may be brought to perfection. Almost all of these spheres of mental activity have as their single goal the inquiry after truth. Were I to set out to extol this inquiry, I would arouse wonder at my eulogizing something that no one ever thought of disparaging.

Let us now scrutinize these advantages of our study meth-ods, and try to ascertain whether these methods lack some of the good qualities possessed by those of antiquity: or whether, instead, they are impaired by faults from which ancient methods were exempt. Let us examine whether we can avoid our deficiencies and appropriate the good points of the ancient methods, and by what means this may be done; and let us see whether those among our deficiencies which are unavoidable may be offset by the shortcomings of antiquity.

III

Let us begin with the *instruments* with which modern sci-ences operate.

Philosophical criticism is the subject which we compel our youths to take up first. Now, such speculative criticism, the main purpose of which is to cleanse its fundamental truths not only of all falsity, but also of the mere suspicion of error, places upon the same plane of falsity not only false thinking, but also those secondary verities and ideas which are based on probability alone, and commands us to clear our minds of them. Such an approach is distinctly harmful, since training in common sense is essential to the education of adolescents, so that that faculty should be developed as early as possible; else they break into odd or arrogant behavior when adulthood is reached. It is a positive fact that, just as knowledge originates in truth and error in falsity, so common sense arises from perceptions based on verisimilitude. Probabilities stand, so to speak, midway between truth and falsity, since things which most of the time are true, are only very seldom false.

Consequently, since young people are to be educated in common sense, we should be careful to avoid that the growth of common sense be stifled in them by a habit of advanced speculative criticism. I may add that common sense, besides being the criterion of practical judgment, is also the guiding standard of eloquence. It frequently occurs, in fact, that orators in a law court have greater difficulty with a case which is based on truth, but does not seem so, than with a case that is false but plausible. There is a danger that instruction in advanced philosophical criticism may lead to an abnormal growth of abstract intellectualism, and render young people unfit for the practice of eloquence.

Our modern advocates of advanced criticism rank the unadulterated essence of "pure," primary truth before, outside, above the gross semblances of physical bodies. But this study of primal philosophical truths takes place at the time when young minds are too immature, too unsure, to derive benefit from it.

Just as old age is powerful in reason, so is adolescence in imagination. Since imagination has always been esteemed a most favorable omen of future development, it should in no

way be dulled. Furthermore, the teacher should give the greatest care to the cultivation of the pupil's memory, which, though
not exactly the same as imagination, is almost identical with
it. In adolescence, memory outstrips in vigor all other faculties, and should be intensely trained. Youth's natural inclination to the arts in which imagination or memory (or a combination of both) is prevalent (such as painting, poetry, oratory, jurisprudence) should by no means be blunted. Nor
should advanced philosophical criticism, the common instrument today of all arts and sciences, be an impediment to any
of them. The Ancients knew how to avoid this drawback. In
almost all their schools for youths, the role of logic was ful-
filled by geometry. Following the example of medical practitioners, who concentrate their efforts on seconding the bent
of Nature, the Ancients required their youths to learn the
science of geometry which cannot be grasped without a vivid
capacity to form images. Thus, without doing violence to
nature, but gradually and gently and in step with the mental
capacities of their age, the Ancients nurtured the reasoning
powers of their young men.

In our days, instead, philosophical criticism alone is honored. The art of "topics," [7] far from being given first place in
the curriculum, is utterly disregarded. Again I say, this is
harmful, since the invention of arguments is by nature prior
to the judgment of their validity, so that, in teaching, that
invention should be given priority over philosophical criticism.
In our days, we keep away from the art of inventing arguments,
and think that this skill is of no use. We hear people affirming
that, if individuals are critically endowed, it is sufficient to
teach them a certain subject, and they will have the capacity
to discover whether there is any truth in that subject. It is
claimed that, without any previous training in the *ars topica,*
any person will be able to discern the probabilities which sur-
round any ordinary topic, and to evaluate them by *the same
standard employed in the sifting of truth.* But who can be sure
that he has taken into consideration every feature of the sub-

[7] See Introduction, note 1, p. xx.

ject on hand? The most eulogizing epithet that can be given
to a speech is that it is "comprehensive": praise is due to the
speaker who has left nothing untouched, and has omitted
nothing from the argument, nothing which may be missed by
his listeners.

Nature and life are full of incertitude; the foremost, indeed,
the only aim of our "arts" is to assure us that we have acted
rightly. Criticism is the art of true speech; "ars topica," of eloquence. Traditional "topics" is the art of finding "the medium," i.e., the middle term: in the conventional language of
scholasticism, "medium" indicates what the Latins call argu-
mentum.[8] Those who know all the loci, i.e., the lines of argument to be used, are able (by an operation not unlike reading
the printed characters on a page) to grasp extemporaneously
the elements of persuasion inherent in any question or case.
Individuals who have not achieved this ability hardly deserve
the name of orators, In pressing, urgent affairs, which do not
admit of delay or postponement, as most frequently occurs
in our law courts—especially when it is a question of criminal
cases, which offer to the eloquent orator the greatest op-
portunity for the display of his powers—it is the orator's
business to give immediate assistance to the accused, who is
usually granted only a few hours in which to plead his defense. Our experts in philosophical criticism, instead, whenever
they are confronted with some dubious point, are wont to
say: "Give me some time to think it over!"

I may add that in the art of oratory the relationship between speaker and listeners is of the essence. It is in tune with
the opinions of the audience that we have to arrange our
speech. It often happens that people unmoved by forceful and
compelling reasons can be jolted from their apathy, and made
to change their minds by means of some trifling line of argument. Consequently, in order to be sure of having touched
all the soul-strings of his listeners, the orator, then, should run
through the complete set of the loci which schematize the

[8] I.e., lines of reasoning along which the discussion of the subject is
to be conducted.

evidence. It is quite unfair to blame Cicero for having in-sisted on many a point of little weight. It was exactly by those points of little weight that he was able to dominate the law courts, the Senate, and (most important of all) the Assemblies of the people. It was by that method that he became the speaker most worthy of being considered a representative of Rome's imperial greatness. It is not significant that it is precisely the orator whose only concern is the bare truth who get stranded in cases in which a different speaker succeeds in extricating himself, by paying attention to credibility as well as the facts? The contrast of opinion between Marcus Brutus and Cicero, regarding the manner in which each of them thought that the defense of Milo should be conducted, pro-vides an instructive case for reflection.

Marcus Brutus, who had been trained in a kind of philo-sophical, rationalistic criticism closely akin to ours (for he was a Stoic), thought that Milo [9] should be defended by throwing his case upon the judges' mercy, and that he should seek ac-quittal on the ground of the distinguished services he had performed for the Republic, and on the ground of having rid Rome of Clodius, a noxious criminal.

Cicero, instead, an expert in the *ars topica*, deemed it un-safe to throw such a defendant upon the judges' indulgence, considering the conditions prevalent at that time. As a conse-quence, he based his defense speech entirely on conjectural reasons. Had he been given the chance of delivering that speech in court, he would certainly have brought about Milo's acquittal, as Milo himself declared.

[9] Titus Annius Milo from Lanuvium. He was appointed tribune of the people in 57 B.C. and was a bitter opponent of the gang-leader Clodius, who, through his gladiators and henchmen, had established a reign of ter-ror in Rome and its environs. Milo, in a battle near Bovillae (now Le Frattocchie) killed Clodius on January 20, 52 B.C. Previously, he had been instrumental in recalling Cicero from exile. Cicero composed a brilliant defense of Milo, but was prevented by fear from delivering it in the Forum. Milo was sent in banishment to Massilia (Marseilles). It is said that, being served an excellent fish meal, Milo ironically said: "Had it not been for Cicero, I would not now be enjoying these splendid mullets."

Nevertheless, Antoine Arnauld,[10] a man of commanding scholarship, scorns the *ars topica,* and considers it of absolutely no use.

Whom shall we believe? Arnauld, who rejects the *ars topica,* or Cicero, who asserts that his own eloquence is chiefly due to the art of skillfully arraying a set of effective lines of argument? Let others decide; as for me, I am unwilling to award to the one what I would have to take away from the other: I shall limit myself to stating that a severely intellectualistic criticism enables us to achieve truth, while *are topica* makes us eloquent. In antiquity, the Stoics devoted themselves entirely to philosophical criticism, while the Academics cultivated topics. Similarly, today the jejune and aridly deductive reasoning in which the Stoics specialized is followed by the moderns, whereas the Aristotelians of the recent past are characterized by the varied and multiform style of their utterance.

An argument presented by Pico della Mirandola, which a learned modern would contract into a single sorites, is rebutted by Cajetan in a string of one hundred syllogisms.[11]

[10] Antoine Arnauld (1612–1694) was, after the death of Saint Cyran, the undisputed leader of Jansenism, and the most unbending adversary of the Jesuits. In the controversy concerning the *Augustinus* of Bishop Cornelius Jansenius, Arnauld defended Jansenius in his *Apologie de M. Jansenius* (1643–1644). Arnauld was the author of the famous distinction between *droit* (law) and *fait* (fact—the Church is not infallible in *questions de fait*). He wrote more than 320 works, the complete edition of which comprises 42 volumes: see *Œuvres de M. Antoine Arnauld,* ed. G. Dupac and J. Hautefage (Lausanne, 1775–1783). Arnauld, in collaboration with Nicole, was the author of the *Port-Royal Logic,* in which, contrary to what Vico states, the *ars topica* is not explicitly attacked. But, says Antonio Corsano, "it is undeniable that the *Art de penser,*" i.e., the *Logique de Port Royal,* "in which the logico-didactic trend of Jansenism is most clearly shown, is dominated by a fierce aversion to any sort of semi-skepticism or probabilism, to any compromise between truth and error: by a disinclination toward that confusion of reality and appearance on which the semi-rational (or altogether irrational) psychological spell of rhetoric is based" (Corsano edn. and trans. of *De nostri, Il metodo degli studi del tempo nostro* [Florence: Vallecchi, 1937]).

[11] Cardinal de Vio (1469–1534), called Gaetanus from his place of birth, Gaeta, was a General of the Dominican Order (1508), one of the most

It is significant that the representatives of the schools of ancient philosophy became the more eloquent in proportion as they were less inclined to a strictly philosophical criticism. The advocates of Stoicism (for whom, as for our *moderni,* pure reason is the regulative standard of truth), were the thinnest and leanest of all philosophers. The Epicureans, according to whom the regulative standard of truth resides in sense-perception, were simple in expression, and unfolded their doctrines in more detail. The ancient Academics instead, being disciples of Socrates who contended that he knew nothing but his own ignorance, were masters of an overflowing and lavishly embellished expression. As for the neo-Academics, who admitted that they did not even know that they did not know anything, they overwhelmed their listeners with torrential outbursts and snowdrifts of oratory.

Both Stoics and Epicureans came out in support of only one side of the argument; Plato inclined towards one or the other side, depending on which appeared to him more probable; Carneades,[12] instead, was wont to embrace both of the

---

outstanding Catholic divines of his age, and a vehement enemy of Luther (De Vio was Apostolic legate to Germany in 1518). He was instrumental in bringing about the election to the imperial office of Charles V (June 28, 1519). De Vio was a prolific theological writer; the complete catalogue of his works is given by Mandonnet in *Dictionnaire de Théologie Catholique* (Paris: Letouizy et Ané, 1909–1950) Vol. II, cols. 1313–1329.

[12] This view of Plato is somewhat akin to that expressed by Montaigne, with whose opinion Vico was probably not acquainted. Carneades of Cyrene (214–129 B.C.) integrated with the doctrine of probabilism the skeptical tradition initiated by Arcesilaus. Carneades went to Rome (together with Critolaus and Diogenes of Seleucia) in 156 B.C. in order to plead the defense of Athens, which the Romans had put under a heavy fine because of the plunder of Oropus. On that occasion, Carneades delivered two speeches, one in favor of justice, and one against it. Cicero (*Republic* III has left us a résumé of them. According to Guido Calogero, Carneades is one of the greatest and most complex figures in the history of ancient philosophy: his epistemological critique reveals an incomparably more rigorous subjectivism than that of Protagoras (article "Carneade," in *Enciclopedia Italiana,* Vol. IX [Rome: Treccani, 1931], p. 96). He was the harshest critic of Stoic epistemology. None of his numerous works is extant, but we know his doctrines through the notes of his disciples, Clitomachus of Carthage and Zeno of Alexandria.

sides of any given controversy. He would, for instance, affirm one day that justice exists, another day, that it does not, bringing forth equally compelling arguments for both positions and displaying an unbelievable power of argumentation. This was due to the fact that whereas truth is *one,* probabilities are many, and falsehoods numberless.

Each procedure, then, has its defects. The specialists in topics fall in with falsehood; the philosophical critics disdain any traffic with probability.

To avoid both defects, I think, young men should be taught the totality of sciences and arts, and their intellectual powers should be developed to the full; thus they will become familiar with the art of argument, drawn from the *ars topica.* At the very outset, their common sense should be strengthened so that they can grow in prudence and eloquence. Let their imagination and memory be fortified so that they may be effective in those arts in which fantasy and the mnemonic faculty are predominant. At a later stage let them learn criticism, so that they can apply the fullness of their personal judgment to what they have been taught. And let them develop skill in debating on either side of any proposed argument.

Were this done, young students, I think, would become exact in science, clever in practical matters, fluent in eloquence, imaginative in understanding poetry or painting, and strong in memorizing what they have learned in their legal studies.

They would not feel the impulse to step rashly into discussions while they are still in process of learning; nor would they, with pedestrian slavishness, refuse to accept any viewpoint unless it has been sanctioned by a teacher. In this sphere, the Ancients seem to me to be superior to us.

A five-year period of silence was enjoined upon all of Pythagoras' students.[13] After that time, they were allowed

---

[13] Pythagoras (*ca.* 580–500 B.C.), born at Samos, settled at Croton in South Italy, and there founded his famous school. The Pythagoreans were dogmatic worshippers of the authority of their master ("he said it"). Pythagoras was a strange combination of philosopher, mathematician,

to maintain what they had learned, but had to ground their reasons only upon the authority of their master. "He said it," was their motto. The chief duty of a student of philosophy was to listen. Most appropriately were they called "auditors."

Arnauld himself, although his words seem to spurn this procedure, actually confirms and professes what I am stating. His treatise on *Logic* [14] is replete with far-fetched and involved illustrations, with difficult examples drawn from the deep storehouses of each discipline. Naturally, these illustrations and examples prove to be unintelligible to the young student, unless he is already more than proficient in those arts and sciences from which those supporting materials are taken, and unless his teacher devotes great efforts and a great deal of eloquent skill to the explanation of them. If logic is studied at the terminal stage of the school curriculum, these deficiencies, besides those I have mentioned before, are avoided. What Arnauld presents, though he provides useful examples, is hardly to be understood; the materials offered by the Aristotelians, instead, though perfectly intelligible, are of no use whatever.[15]

---

scientist, and mystic. Some of the precepts of his school were even more curious than that quoted by Vico (such is, for instance, the prohibition of eating horse beans). Pythagoras exerted a great influence on Plato.

[14] This is the famous *Art de penser,* also entitled *Logique de Port Royal,* co-authored by Antoine Arnauld and Pierre Nicole (1625–1695), and published in 1662. Cartesian influence on French education found in the *Port-Royal Logic* one of its most efficient vehicles. It has been noted that the analysis of language *qua* logical expression takes its starting point from this book. In Vico's Naples, the *Port-Royal Logic* had found enthusiastic endorsement on the part of the "innovators" (the pro-Cartesians), and had been scornfully rejected by the Jesuits (see Vincenzo de Ruvo edn. of *De nostri,* translated into Italian, with Introduction and notes [Padua: Cedam, 1941]).

[15] The Aristotelians referred to here were, according to Corsano, the Schoolmen, authors of the so-called *Summulae Logicales.* Nicolini mentions, among them, Petrus Hispanus (1226–1276), Paolo Nicoletti da Udine (1372–*ca.* 1429), whom Vico calls "the sharpest-minded of all composers of *Summulae.*" Fausto Nicolini, edn. of *De nostri,* Vol. I (1914) of Vico's *Opere* (Laterza: Bari, 1914–1941).

IV

We now come to the problems raised by the applications made by the moderns of the geometrical method to physics. Here we meet with the following difficulty.

It is impossible to discard any part of the deductive process, unless one attacks that method's basic principle. Consequently, only three courses of action remain open. The first is to unlearn this type of physics based on geometry, and resort to a non-scientific contemplation of the cosmos. The second: if it is decided that the modern kind of physics should be adhered to, then a new method could be devised to frame it. Third: we may retain our present method, and endeavor to account for any new phenomenon as a corollary to this modern type of physics. (I may say, in this connection, that our modern physicists remind me of certain individuals who have inherited from their parents a gorgeous mansion leaving nothing to be desired in point of comfort or luxury. There is nothing left for them to do except to move the furniture around, and by slight modifications, add some ornaments and bring things up to date.)

However, in the opinion of our scientists, that type of physics which they teach, based on the geometrical method, is, as it were, the authentic voice of Nature. Wherever you turn in contemplating the universe, you will constantly be met by the ever-present modern physics. We owe a tremendous debt of gratitude, modern scientists say, to those geniuses who have freed us from the burdensome task of speculating on nature, and who have bequeathed to us such wealthy and luxuriously furnished mansions. If it is true that the structure and functions of the cosmos are exactly as they describe them, then let those scientific pioneers be most fervently thanked. But if Nature is organized differently—if a single one of the laws of motion established by our modern physicists is false (not to mention that already more than one has been proved false),[16] let our enthusiasts pause and repeatedly ponder whether they are not carelessly following an unsafe path, leading away from the goal of the solution of the problems of nature. It may happen that, while they are trying to repair the roof of the mansion, they may, at their peril, pay too little attention to the foundations.

Let us not deceive either others or ourselves. In the geometrical field, these deductive methods, these sorites, are excellent ways and means of demonstrating mathematical truths. But, whenever the subject matter is unsuited to deductive treatment, the geometrical procedure may be a faulty and captious way of reasoning. For this reason the ancient philosophical schools censured the Stoics, who used this method of demonstrating mathematical truths. The Ancients fought rather shy of the logic of Chrysippus [17] (which was predomi-

---

[10] For a commentary on this passage, the reader is referred to Paul Mouy, *Les lois du choc des corps d'après Malebranche* (Paris: J. Vrin, 1927). Corsano points out that, as early as 1699, Leibniz had demonstrated that the second and third Cartesian laws concerning the clash of physical bodies were inexact (see Yvon Belaval on *Leibniz critique de Descartes* [Paris: Gallimard, 1960]). Interesting in this connection are the remarks by Carlini. Because of their importance, they deserve to be set down here: "The third Cartesian law concerns the change of the quantity of motion present in two clashing bodies. This is the part which, by neglecting concrete elements and factors in the mechanics of bodies (elasticity, mass, potential energy, etc), pre-eminently shows the abstractness of the purely geometrical and cinematic considerations of Descartes. In his view, force is reduced to the concept of the pressure of a surface on another surface. The absence of dynamic principle caused the decline of Cartesian physical theory when confronted with the new Newtonian physics" (A. Carlini, *Il problema di Cartesio* [Bari: Laterza, 1948]). See also Paul Mouy, *Le développement de la physique cartésienne* (Paris: J. Vrin, 1934).

[17] The dialectical power and subtlety of reasoning of Chrysippus (born in Cilicia, *ca.* 280 B.C.) was, in antiquity, proverbial. He was the most important organizer of the Stoic school. His productivity as a philosophical writer is appalling: 705 books! The finest modern monograph on Chrysippus is that by Émile Bréhier, the noted historian of philosophy: *Chrysippe* (Paris: F. Alcan, 1910). The extant fragments of Chrysippus are gathered in H. V. Arnim, ed., *Stoicorum veterum fragmenta*, IV (Lipsaie:

nantly deductive), and thought it decidedly insidious and deceptive.

As a consequence, the principles of physics which are put forward as truths on the strength of the geometrical method are not really truths, but wear a semblance of probability. The method by which they were reached is that of geometry, but physical truths so elicited are not demonstrated as reliably as are geometrical axioms. We are able to demonstrate geometrical propositions because we create them; were it possible for us to supply demonstrations of propositions of physics, we would be capable of creating them *ex nihilo* as well.

The archetypal *forms,* the ideal patterns of reality, exist in God alone. The physical nature of things, the phenomenal world, is modeled after those archetypes.[18] It is our task to study physics in a speculative temper of mind, as philosophers, that is, curbing our presumption. Let us surpass the Ancients; they pursued researches in nature in order to match the gods in happiness; we should, instead, cultivate the study of physics in order to curb our pride. Intensely ambitious as we are to attain truth, let us engage upon its quest. Where we fail in

---

B. G. Teubner [1903–1924]). Nicolini rightly surmises that Vico's allusion is to the discussion of Chrysippus' sophisms, which appears in Cicero's *Academica.*

[18] In the history of Western thought, this theory first appears in the writings of the early Fathers of the Church. They saw their doctrinal task as that of blending Christianity and Platonism. Plato had asserted the distinction between archetypes (archetypal ideas, *paradeigmata*) and images (individual objects, *eidola*). "The early Fathers of the Church found it easier to Christianize Plato's philosophy than did Albertus Magnus and St. Thomas to do the like for Aristotle. They unanimously understood Plato to locate the world of ideas in the mind of God, and they explained the *cosmos noetòs* as a system of divine conceptions, of archetypes, according to which God was to form . . . the various species of created things. The *locus classicus* stating this position is one by St. Augustine (*De divinatione,* Q. XIVI): Ideas are certain original forms of things, their archetypes, permanent and immutable, which are contained in the divine intelligence. And though they neither begin to be or cease, yet upon them are patterned the manifold things of the world which come into being or pass away." ("Idealism," in *Catholic Encyclopedia* [New York: D. Appleton Co., 1910], Vol. VII, p. 634.)

this quest, our very longing will lead us as by the hand towards the Supreme Being, who alone is the Truth, and the
Path and Guide to it.

It should be added that the geometrical method constitutes
a hindrance in the way of an eloquent exposition of the principles of physics. The geometrical method enables us to set
forth matters in a purely geometrical, apodeictic form, and
gives us the possibility of teaching them in a plain, unadorned
way, devoid of any aesthetic charm. All of the modern physicists affect a style of exposition which is as severe as it is limited. Our theory of physics (in the process of learning as well
as when mastered) moves forward by a constant and gradual
series of small, closely concatenated steps. Consequently, it
is apt to smother the student's specifically philosophic faculty,
i.e., his capacity to perceive the analogies existing between
matters lying far apart and, apparently, most dissimilar. It
is this capacity which constitutes the source and principle of
all ingenious, acute, and brilliant forms of expression. It
should be emphasized that tenuity, subtlety, delicacy of
thought, is not identical with acuity of ideas. That which is
tenuous, delicately refined, may be represented by a single
line; "acute" by two.[19] Metaphor, the greatest and brightest
ornament of forceful, distinguished speech, undoubtedly plays
the first role in acute, figurative expression.

But there is also another reason why those who are accus-
tomed to the geometrical kind of exposition are less capable of conveying their ideas with eloquence. It is to the
modes of thinking of an ignorant multitude that eloquence

[19] The best interpretation of this passage has been given by Ruvo, in
his edn. of *De nostri* (p. 25, note 2): in a "subtle" piece of reasoning, the
argument runs, as it were, along a thread of logic, from one truth to another; whereas "acuteness" is the convergence of two kinds of considerations: the one, aiming at understanding the particular in relation to
the universal truth; the other, aiming at viewing the particular exclusively in its contingency. The two kinds of considerations may be likened
to two convergent visual rays, focusing and bestowing preciseness upon
the concrete aspects of a particular fact.

is particularly suited. Men with no tincture of letters find it extremely difficult to follow a long chain of reasoning—to catch, especially,

> words that are flying, and cannot ever be recaptured.

Even if it were possible for an uncultivated audience to follow a speaker's rapid pace of delivery, it would still be inadvisable for the orator to overtax the attention of his listeners by imposing on them an intense effort. Therefore, when an orator addresses such a gathering, he should adopt a free, ample manner of utterance. He should now prove a point, now embark on an incidental digression, now revert to his theme, now bestow a more elegant and neater turn upon what he has roughly blocked out, now enlarge on points sketchily grazed, now give a more assertive tone to what he has superficially treated. At times he should pause on a single point and stress it, drawing now upon one of the oratorical figures, now upon another, so that the listener may take it home, deeply stamped upon his soul.

I would finally have you notice that the modern physicists, in the application of their method, proceed by placing primary axioms first. The skillful orator, instead, omits things that are well known, and while impressing on his hearers secondary truth, he tacitly reminds them of the primal points he has left out and while he carries through his argument, his listeners are made to feel that they are completing it themselves. This is the way in which the orator stirs their minds before he sets about arousing their emotions. A shape, however beautiful, cannot by itself draw a unanimous response. But the pleasure imparted by an excellent speaker pleases everybody without exception.

I have, now, in the application of the geometrical method to physics, indicated how the drawbacks can be remedied. I have already said something in regard to the shortcomings of philosophical criticism, and how to avoid them. A few additional remarks will come later.

V

Let us now proceed to "analysis." It must be frankly admitted that the most learned among the Ancients possessed no more ability to solve the problems of geometry than did Davus; we moderns, by the help of our methods, have attained the ingenuity of Oedipus.[20] However, in view of the fact that facility enervates, whereas difficulty sharpens the mind, we must stop to inquire whether modern discoveries in mechanics should be credited to "analysis," or not.

To contribute new inventions is a characteristic feature of an ingenious mind alone: and undoubtedly ingeniousness is kept in training by geometry. Just as the horse-trainer pulls

[20] Davus is the slow-witted servant of Simo in Terence's *Lady of Andros;* Vico's reference is to dialogue between them in Act I, scene 1. Oedipus is the most skilled decipherer of deep riddles. What Vico means is that "analysis" (i.e., algebraic procedure) has given to us moderns, *qua* decipherers of the enigmas of geometry, an enormous advantage over the Ancients. It is well known that the discovery of analytic geometry by Descartes was occasioned by the stimulus provided by Golius' invitation to unriddle the Pappus problem, left unsolved by the Ancients, a problem which Descartes brilliantly unties in his *Geometry.* Vico's designation of analytical geometry by the term "analysis" is absolutely correct, since, as Étienne Gilson points out, analytical geometry is nothing but an application of the precept of analysis to the study of geometrical curves. Says Gilson: "In effect, the system of right-angle coordinates [Cartesian coordinates] allows us to express geometrical relationships under the form of algebraic equations, a procedure which leads to the *simplification* advocated by Descartes: a system of relationships studied on straight lines and expressible algebraically. Moreover, all the geometrical curves are, by now, made to fall within a single class, wherein they arrange themselves by kinds, according to the degree of their equation (*Geometry,* Book II, chap. 6). Thus, the precept which urges us to take our point of departure, always, from the most simple, in order to rise, in orderly fashion, to the more complex, becomes applicable to all geometrical curves which may now be studied, thanks to the new procedure championed by Descartes" (René Descartes, *Discours de la méthode,* Text and Commentary by Étienne Gilson [Paris: J. Vrin, 1925], p. 190).

his animal slightly short, in order that it may develop greater speed in racing, so geometry holds in check the reasoning powers of the learner, in order that, when recalled to use, those powers may prove most penetrating. "Analysis" (i.e., analytical geometry) confronts the student with a wealth of notational signs, so that, like a reader scanning at a glance the characters on a page of writing, he may run swiftly through the whole series of those graphic symbols and, by reading and assembling them, may find the solution to the problem on hand. Like the

> oracular priestess who, still resisting Phoebus,
> raves in great fury, and fiercely struggles
> to shake off the god from her breast,
>
> [Vergil, *Aeneid* VI. 77–79]

analysis rapidly casts up its own great reckonings, waiting for the moment when it will discover, perhaps by chance, the long-sought equation which supplies the key to the solution of the problem.[21]

Geometry is undoubtedly a propulsive force in the development of mechanical inventions. It is stated that during the

[21] It is superfluous to point out that Vico's view of the process leading to the finding of the equation is utterly fanciful. Analytical geometry was not the product of the Dionysiac inspiration of a single hierophant of mathematics. As Carl B. Boyer phrases it: "Few new branches of mathematics are the work of single individuals. The analytic geometry of Descartes was certainly not the result of their investigations only, but was the outgrowth of several mathematical trends which converged in the sixteenth and seventeenth centuries. It was the result of the influence of Apollonius, Oresme, Viète, and many others" (Carl B. Boyer, *History of the Calculus and Its Conceptual Development* [New York: Dover Publications, 1949], p. 187). In Vico's extenuation, it may be pleaded that, as Boyer further remarks, the spirit of the seventeenth century (Vico: 1668–1744), to which, in this respect, Vico still belongs, was "directed towards the solution of problems through geometrical [not analytical] considerations." Such an "arithmetization of mathematics" (i.e., analytical geometry) was opposed with particular vigor by two Englishmen, the philosopher Thomas Hobbes and the mathematician and theologian Isaac Barrow. Hobbes objected strenuously to "the whole herd of them who apply their algebra to geometry" (Boyer, p. 175).

siege of Syracuse the great geometrician Archimedes invented
the most marvelous machines of war.[22] Some, however, have
suggested that he had already invented the analytical method
of geometry and that, driven by spite, had kept the secret
to himself. The motive of those making this insinuation may
be, perhaps, a desire to magnify verbally their own contributions (no small gift) to the common fund of our knowledge. Nevertheless it is undeniable that the inventions made
in modern times, in which we are so immeasurably superior
to the Ancients, such as (to mention a few), the cannon, the
ship propelled by sails alone, the clock, suspended church-
domes, antedate the time when "analysis" became a routine
procedure. No one, however ardent a defender of the
Ancients, would be reluctant to admit that by the invention of the clock we have immeasurably outdone the ingenuity of the men of past epochs. The ships of antiquity,
including those propelled by sixteen banks of oars, were
rather gorgeous affairs, but very cumbersome. Our ships, instead, fitted with sails alone, have true power.

What I am saying about ships applies also to the grandiose
siege-machines of Demetrius Poliorcetes,[23] and to other war-
engines of antiquity. It may be said that the marvels of Mem-
phis and other miracles of antiquity, in which some trace of

[22] Archimedes, born *ca.* 287 B.C. in Syracuse, was the most important
mathematician, physicist, machine-builder, and theorist of mechanics of
antiquity. During the Second Punic War, he defended his native city
against the Romans for two years, while in his seventies. A soldier killed
him, when the city was conquered, at a moment when Archimedes was
trying to solve a mathematical problem. Marcellus, the general who commanded the Roman forces, had issued a special command to spare him.

[23] Demetrius Poliorcetes (*ca.* 337–283 B.C.), "the type of the Macedonian
condottiere," participated actively in the succession struggles following the
death of Alexander the Great. "Poliorcetes" means "city besieger"; he
distinguished himself by applying to the beleaguering of cities warfare
techniques which, in his time, were considered quite advanced. Famous in
this respect is his siege of Rhodes (305–304 B.C.). The reader is urged to
consult the splendid essay of Jakob Burckhardt entitled "Demetrius, der
Staedtebezwinger," in Burckhardt's academic *Vorträge, 1884–1887,* ed. Emil
Dürr (3 vols.; Basil: B. Schwabe, 1919). Plutarch wrote a life of Demetrius.

superiority of the Ancients over us may be discerned, were rather ostentatious specimens of ancient manual labor than feats of eminent engineering skill.

Take, instead, an outstanding achievement of modern architectural technique: the suspended church-dome, declared impossible by Architecture itself. Consider the ordeals, the tribulations, which Filippo Brunelleschi, who in the church of Santa Maria del Fiore first dared to undertake, and to accomplish this feat, was made to suffer at the hands of his fellow architects! [24] Brunelleschi's rivals stubbornly maintained that it was absolutely impossible that even the smallest weight— let alone that immense bulk of masonry reaching aloft into the immensity of the sky—could be erected on four pendant points; and yet it was done.

Is there no significance to the fact that those scientists who contributed new and spectacular inventions in mechanics, after analytical geometry had become a current practice, clearly despised that geometrical method? And that those who strove to invent some machine relying on "analysis" alone met with constant failure? The case of P. Perot is in point. He built a ship the proportions of which had been carefully calculated beforehand according to the rules of analytical geometry, expecting it to be the swiftest vessel in existence. But as soon as the ship slid from the docks into the water, it sank to the bottom of the sea and remained there as motionless as a rock.

Perhaps the reason is that, just as pieces of music composed in accordance with a mathematical formula give no pleasure, so machines built according to the principles of analytical geom-

24 The tribulations of Filippo Brunelleschi (1377–1446), the initiator of Renaissance architecture, inventor of linear perspective, sculptor, builder of the dome of Santa Maria del Fiore, are minutely recounted in Giorgio Vasari's *Lives of the Eminent Painters* . . . (several translations available). A competent modern account of the plan and construction of the cupola has been given by P. Sampaolesi, *La cupola di Santa Maria del Fiore* (Rome: La Costruzione, 1941). The cupola was begun in 1420 and finished in 1434. An extremely fine interpretation of Brunelleschi's achievements is contained in G. C. Argan, *Brunelleschi* (Milan: Mondadori, 1955).

etry are of no practical use. This is not part of our discussion. But we may ask whether those among the moderns who have enriched mechanics with inventions have not done so by the conjunction of their own ingenuity with the power of Euclidian geometry, rather than by any application of analysis.

It may be inferred from this that we need to train young minds for the practice of mechanics by means of a close study of visual geometrical figures, and not by means of abstract algebraic symbols. Analytical procedure is, so to speak, a kind of art of divination; we should resort to it as to a god *ex machina,* and not

> allow the god to intervene, unless the plot
> deserves to be unraveled by such a supernatural
> character.
>   [Horace, *Ars poetica* 191–192]

VI

Medicine is handicapped by drawbacks incident to the fact that, while we are aware that our knowledge of the causes of disease is not reliable, we pay scanty attention to symptoms, and make diagnoses rashly. Since the Ancients were superior to us in these respects, their techniques and theory of medicine were more trustworthy. They felt that the causes of disease are deeply hidden and uncertain; as a consequence, they were exacting and scrupulous in their effort to aim at the only result which they knew they could, on the basis of a long-continued observation, aim at and achieve; and this result was to get hold, not so much of the causes as of the symptoms of disease, and then surmise the disease's gravity and future course, and proceed to conduct a medical treatment.

Observe, in this connection, the remarkable parallelism existing between physical and mental illness. Courtiers are not only ignorant of the nature of the anger of the ruler, but also of the impulses which cause him to become angry. Yet, taught by experience, they can anticipate the moment when their master may burst into anger, and avoid crossing him; they also may be able to foretell what degree of intensity that fit of anger will reach, and take care not to inflame their master further. They know at what point the ruler's anger will subside, so as to bring about in him a mood of forgiveness, and at what point his indignation is utterly extinguished, so as to insinuate themselves again, with soft words, into his favor.

Today, no dictum is more current with the generality of physicians than: "Let us suspend action, and wait for the disease to come to a head." This dictum, and the attitude it indicates, was unknown to the Ancients. They realized that physical health, like everything else that is good, can be more easily preserved than restored. They watched sedulously those intimations of future disease which a healthy body may give out, so that the illness might be provided against and prevented.

A particularly enthusiastic proponent of this method of treatment was Tiberuis, the Roman emperor.[25] He felt that all men, on reaching their thirties, should be counted upon to have mastered the art of medicine. The Romans, who had practiced it for centuries, were signally expert at it. And, in truth, one's own nature will not be insidious to any one, but with loyalty and unremitting vigilance will keep guard over the health of each one of us. Unfailingly, before being attacked by disease, the body gives us, by some symptom, a premonition of its impending ordeal, and, maybe, of its future

[25] Emperor Tiberius (Julius Caesar) lived from 41 B.C. to A.D. 37. He was the son of Livia, Augustus' wife, by a prior marriage. Augustus named him his heir in A.D. 14, when Tiberius was 55 years of age, and he reigned from 14 to 37. He fought the Germanic tribes, quelled the insurrection of the Sarmatians and Pannonians, and, during the latter part of his rule, became a monster of cruelty. Vico's reference is based on the following passage of Suetonius: "He enjoyed excellent health, which was all but perfect during nearly the whole of his reign, although from his thirtieth year he took care of it according to his own ideas, without the aid or advice of physicians" (Suetonius, *Lives of the Caesars*, trans. J. C. Rolfe [Cambridge: The Loeb Classical Library, 1960], Vol. I, p. 391). F. Nicolini remarks that Vico is quoting by memory, and slightly modifies the content of Suetonius' passage.

wreckage. It is we who fail in the art of caring for ourselves, and pay no heed; so that it may be said that just as no great event happens all of a sudden, so nobody really dies of a sudden death.

To obviate the main drawbacks of our art of medicine, let me elaborate on the causes which I have barely indicated just now. Today, having made the discovery of a single truth, we proceed to draw from it a whole series of inferences concerning the phenomena of Nature. But symptoms and judgments, drawn from long-continued observation, are merely probable approximations to truth. Francis Bacon charges that the followers of Galen, who employ the syllogism, reach wrong conclusions concerning the causes of disease. Like Bacon, I would maintain that the moderns are led astray by their fondness for that strictly deductive form of reasoning which the Greeks called *sorites*. The person who uses the syllogism brings no new element, since the conclusion is already implied in the initial proposition or assumption: analogously, those who employ the sorites merely unfold the secondary truth which lies within the primary statement. Now illnesses are always new and different, and no two sick people are ever alike. Nor am I, at the present moment, the same individual I was but a minute ago while talking of the sick: countless life-instants have already passed by, numberless motions have already taken place, by which I am continuously pushed in the direction of my last day. Thus, since every genus (and every true genus contains a whole series of particular cases) contains an exceedingly great number of specific diseases, and these diseases cannot all be categorized under a single general class name, it is impossible for us to attain truth in this sphere, either through the syllogism, since its major premise consists of a general notion (and particular instances cannot be subsumed under a general notion), or through the strictly deductive procedure of the sorites.

In medicine it would be safer to adhere to concrete particulars, and to refrain from assigning to the sorites a role more important than that which, in this field, it deserves to play; it would be safest to lean firmly on induction. In the investigation of morbific causes, we may incline more to the moderns, because they are clearer in the explanation of causes than the Ancients. But we should pay a great deal of attention to symptoms and diagnostics. Let us cultivate the practices of preventive medicine as applied by the Ancients, chiefly gymnastics and dietetics, along with the curative procedures devised by us.

VII

But the greatest drawback of our educational methods is that we pay an excessive amount of attention to the natural sciences and not enough to ethics. Our chief fault is that we disregard that part of ethics which treats of human character, of its dispositions, its passions, and of the manner of adjusting these factors to public life and eloquence. We neglect that discipline which deals with the differential features of the virtues and vices, with good and bad behavior-patterns, with the typical characteristics of the various ages of man, of the two sexes, of social and economic class, race and nation, and with the art of seemly conduct in life, the most difficult of all arts. As a consequence of this neglect, a noble and important branch of studies, i.e., the science of politics, lies almost abandoned and untended.

Since, in our time, the only target of our intellectual endeavors is truth, we devote all our efforts to the investigation of physical phenomena, because their nature seems unambiguous; but we fail to inquire into human nature which, because of the freedom of man's will, is difficult to determine. A serious drawback arises from the uncontrasted preponderance of our interest in the natural sciences.

Our young men, because of their training, which is focused on these studies, are unable to engage in the life of the community, to conduct themselves with sufficient wisdom and prudence; nor can they infuse into their speech a familiarity with human psychology or permeate their utterances with passion. When it comes to the matter of prudential behavior in life, it is well for us to keep in mind that human events are dominated by Chance and Choice, which are extremely subject to change and which are strongly influenced by simulation and dissimulation (both pre-eminently deceptive things). As a consequence, those whose only concern is abstract truth experience great difficulty in achieving their means, and greater difficulty in attaining their ends. Frustrated in their own plans, deceived by the plans of others, they often throw up the game. Since, then, the course of action in life must consider the importance of the single events and their circumstances, it may happen that many of these circumstances are extraneous and trivial, some of them bad, some even contrary to one's goal. It is therefore impossible to assess human affairs by the inflexible standard of abstract right; we must rather gauge them by the pliant Lesbic rule, which does not conform bodies to itself, but adjusts itself to their contours.

The difference, therefore, between abstract knowledge and prudence is this: in science, the outstanding intellect is that which succeeds in reducing a large multitude of physical effects to a single cause; in the domain of prudence, excellence is accorded to those who ferret out the greatest possible number of causes which may have produced a single event, and who are able to conjecture which of all these causes is the true one. Abstract knowledge—science—is concerned with the highest verity; common sense, instead, with the lowliest. On the basis of this, the distinguished features of the various types of men should be marked out: the fool, the astute ignoramus, the learned man destitute of prudence, and the sage. In the conduct of life the fool, for instance, pays no attention to the highest or the meanest truths; the astute ignoramus notices the meanest but is unable to perceive the highest; the man who is learned but destitute of prudence, deduces the lowest truths from the highest; the sage, instead, derives the highest truths from the unimportant ones. Abstract, or general truths are eternal; concrete or specific ones change momentarily from truths to untruths. Eternal truths stand above nature; in nature, instead, everything is unstable, mutable. But congruity exists between goodness and truth; they partake of the same essence, of the same qualities. Accordingly, the fool, who is ignorant of both general and particular truths, constantly suffers prompt penalties for his arrogance. The astute ignoramus, who is able to grasp particular truths but incapable of conceiving a general truth, finds that cleverness, which is useful to him today, may be harmful to him tomorrow. The learned but imprudent individual, traveling in a straight line from general truths to particular ones, bulls his way through the tortuous paths of life. But the sage who, through all the obliquities and uncertainties of human actions and events, keeps his eye steadily focused on eternal truth, manages to follow a roundabout way whenever he cannot travel in a straight line, and makes decisions, in the field of action, which, in the course of time, prove to be as profitable as the nature of things permits.

Therefore, it is an error to apply to the prudent conduct of life the abstract criterion of reasoning that obtains in the domain of science. A correct judgment deems that men—who are, for the most part, but fools—are ruled, not by forethought, but by whim or chance. The doctrinaires judge human actions as they *ought* to be, not as they actually are (i.e., performed more or less at random). Satisfied with abstract truth alone, and not being gifted with common sense, unused to following probability, those doctrinaires do not bother to find out whether their opinion is held by the generality and whether the things that are truths to them are also such to other people.

This failure to concern themselves with the opinions of others has not only been a source of blame, but has proved to be extremely prejudicial, not only to private persons but to eminent leaders and great rulers as well. Let an example which is right to the point be quoted here: While the assembly of the French Estates was in session, Henry III, King of France, ordered Duke Henry de Guise, a very popular member of the French aristocracy, to be put to death, in spite of the fact that the Duke was under the protection of a safe conduct. Although just cause underlay that order of the king, such cause was not made manifest. The case having been brought up in Rome, Cardinal Ludovico Madruzzi, a man of great judgment in public affairs, commented: "Rulers should see to it not only that their actions are true and in conformity with justice, but that they also *seem* to be so."

Madruzzi's statement was proved true by the calamities which overtook France shortly after.[26]

The Romans, who were great experts in political matters, paid particular attention to appearances. Both their judges and their senators, on giving out an opinion, were always wont to say: "It seems."

To summarize: It was because of their knowledge of the greatest affairs that philosophers were, by the Greeks, called "politici," i.e., experts in matters bearing on the total life of the body politic. Subsequently, philosophers were called Peri-

---

[26] Henri de Lorraine, third Duke of Guise (1550–1588), a nephew of Charles de Guise, Cardinal of Lorraine, was murdered by Henri III of France. The background of this murder is lucidly epitomized in the article devoted to him in the *Columbia Encyclopedia* (3rd edn.; New York: Columbia University Press, 1963), p. 886: "Henri fought on the Catholic side in the wars of religion, and co-operated with Catherine de' Medici in planning the massacre of Saint Bartholomew's day. After the peace of 1576 he formed the Catholic League, of which Henri III, though secretly fearing it, became the nominal head. After the death of Francis, duke of Alençon (1584), Henri de Lorraine revived (1585) the League in opposition to Henri of Navarre, the heir presumptive (later, King Henri IV). Guise, as the defender of the Catholic faith, became immensely popular and overshadowed the King, upon whom he attempted to force the complete program of the League. He instigated the revolt of the Parisians against the King on the Day of the Barricades (May 12, 1588), and took control of the city. He subsequently became reconciled to the King, who, however, brought about his assassination."

Ludovico Madruzzi (1532–1600), born in Trent, was a legate to the Diet of Augsburg; was ambassador to France; in 1561, was appointed cardinal. He took an active part in the Council of Trent, and was several times papal legate to Germany. His personal prestige and influence were deeply felt during the seventh Conclave.

patetics and Academics, these names being derived from two small sections of the town of Athens, where their schools stood. Among the Ancients, the teaching of rational, physical, and ethical doctrines was entrusted to philosophers who took good care to adjust those doctrines to the practical common sense that should govern human behavior.

Today, on the contrary, we seem to have reverted to the type of physical research which was typical of pre-Socratic times.

There was an epoch when the "fourfold philosophy" (i.e., logic, physics, metaphysics, and ethics was handed down by its teachers in a manner fitted to foster eloquence: i.e., the attempt was made to fuse philosophy with eloquence. Demosthenes was a product of the Lyceum; Cicero, of the Academy: there is no doubt that they were the two foremost speakers of the two most splendid of languages. Today, those branches of philosophical theory are taught by such a method as to dry up every fount of convincing expression, of copious, penetrating, embellished, lucid, developed, psychologically effective, and impassionate utterance. The listeners' minds undergo a process of constriction, so as to assume the shape of those young virgins,

. . . whom their mothers compel to bend their
shoulders, to stoop, to bind their bosom
in order to achieve slimness;   ·
if one of the girls is fleshier, they call her "the boxer"
and stint her on food;
if by nature she is healthy, they reduce her, by a special cure,
to the slenderness of a reed.

                        [Terence, *The Eunuch* II.iii.23–26]

Here some learned pundit might object that, in the conduct of life, I would have our young students become courtiers, and not philosophers; pay little attention to truth and follow not reality but appearances; and cast down morality and put on a deceitful "front" of virtue.

I have no such intention. Instead, I should like to have

them act as philosophers, even at court; to care for truth that both is and has the appearance of truth, and to follow that which is morally good and which everybody approves.

As for eloquence, the same men assert that the modern study methods, far from being detrimental, are most useful to it. "How much preferable it is," they say, "to induce persuasion by solid arguments based on truth, to produce such an effect on the mind that, once that truth coalesces with reason, it can never again be separated from it, rather than to coerce the listener's soul by meretriciously eloquent allurements, by blazes of oratorical fire which, as soon as they are extinguished, cause him to revert to his original disposition!"

The answer is that eloquence does not address itself to the rational part of our nature, but almost entirely to our passions. The rational part in us may be taken captive by a net woven of purely intellectual reasonings, but the passional side of our nature can never be swayed and overcome unless this is done by more sensuous and materialistic means. The role of eloquence is to persuade; an orator is persuasive when he calls forth in his hearers the mood which he desires. Wise men induce this condition in themselves by an act of volition. This volition, in perfect obedience, follows the dictates of their intellect; consequently, it is enough for the speaker to point their duty to such wise men, and they do it. But the multitude, the *vulgus,* are overpowered and carried along by their appetite, which is tumultuous and turbulent; their soul is tainted, having contracted a contagion from the body, so that it follows the nature of the body, and is not moved except by bodily things. Therefore, the soul must be enticed by corporeal images and impelled to love; for once it loves, it is easily taught to believe; once it believes and loves, the fire of passion must be infused into it so as to break its inertia and force it to *will.* Unless the speaker can compass these three things, he has not achieved the effect of persuasion; he has been powerless to convince.

Two things only are capable of turning to good use the agitations of the soul, those evils of the inward man which spring from a single source: desire. One is philosophy, which acts to mitigate passions in the soul of the sage, so that those passions are transformed into virtues; the other is eloquence, which kindles these passions in the common sort, so that they perform the duties of virtue.

It may be objected that the form of government under which we live at present no longer allows eloquence to exercise its control over free peoples. To which I answer that we ought to be thankful to our monarchs for governing us not by fist but by laws. However, even under the republican form of government, orators have gained distinction by their fluent, broad, impassioned style of delivery in the law courts, the assemblies, and the religious convocations, to the greatest advantage of the state, and to the signal enrichment of our language.

But let us approach what may be a basic point. The French language is abundantly endowed with words designating abstract ideas. Now, abstraction is in itself but a dull and inert thing, and does not allow the comparative degree. This makes it impossible for the French to impart an ardently emotional tone to their ideas, inasmuch as such an effect can only be achieved by setting thought in motion, and a vehement motion at that; nor can they amplify or elevate their discourse. Nor can they invert the order of words: the conceptual abstraction being the most general category, it does not supply us with that "middle term" where the extreme points of a metaphor are able to meet and unite. It is therefore impossible in French for a single noun to be the vehicle of a metaphor; and metaphors composed of two nouns are, as a rule, somewhat stilted. Furthermore, when the French writers attempt the periodic style, they are unable to get very far, on account of the shortness of the sentence segments. Nor can French poets compose lines of greater breadth than those which are called "alexandrines"; and these alexandrines, besides consisting of two symmetrical portions, are more dragging and spindly than the Latin elegiac lines. (Each verse contains a simple thought, and they rhyme in pairs; the first feature reduces their scope, the second impairs their gravity.) French words have only two kinds of stress; they are accented on the ultima and on the penult, whereas Italian stresses the antepenult. In French the accent shifts to the penult, which results in a somewhat tenuous and thin sound. For these reasons, French is not fit for stately prose, nor for sublime verse. But though the French language cannot rise to any great sublimity or splendor, it is admirably suited to the subtle style. Rich in substantives, especially those denoting what the Scholastics call abstract essences, the French language can always condense into a small compass the essentials of things. Since arts and sciences are mostly concerned with general notions, French is therefore splendidly suited to the didactic genre. While we Italians praise our orators for fluency, lucidity, and eloquence, the French praise theirs for reasoning truly. Whenever the French wish to designate the mental faculty by which we rapidly, aptly, and felicitously couple things which stand apart, they call it *esprit,* and are inclined to view as a naive, simple trick what we consider as forceful power of combination; their minds, characterized by exceeding penetration, do not excel in synthetic power, but in piercing subtlety of reasoning. Consequently, if there is any truth in this statement, which is the theme of a famous debate, "genius is a product of language, not language of genius," we must recognize that the French are the only people who, thanks to the subtlety of their language, were able to invent the new philosophical criticism which seems so thoroughly intellectualistic, and analytical geometry, by which the subject matter of mathematics is, as far as possible, stripped of all concrete, figural elements, and reduced to pure rationality. The French are in the habit of praising the kind of eloquence which characterizes their language, i.e., an eloquence characterized by great fidelity to truth and subtlety, as well as by its notable deductive order. We Italians, instead, are endowed with a language which constantly evokes images. We stand far above other nations by our achievements in the fields of painting, sculpture, architecture, and music. Our language, thanks to its perpetual dynamism, forces the attention of the listeners by means of metaphorical expressions, and prompts it to move back and forth between ideas which are far apart. In the keenness of their perception, the Italians are second only to the Spaniards. Theirs is a language which, in the rich and elevated style (i.e., that of Herodotus, Livy, and Cicero), possesses a Guicciardini; in the grand and vehement style of Thucydides, Demosthenes, and Sallust, it has others; in Attic elegance, it has Boccaccio; in the new lyric style, Petrarch. Ariosto, in the grandeur of his plots and the ease of his diction, puts one in mind of Homer; while a poet like Tasso, by the enchantingly musical sublimity of his rhyme, comes fully up to Virgil. Shall we then not cultivate a language possessing such felicitous qualities?

In conclusion: whosoever intends to devote his efforts, not to physics or mechanics, but to a political career, whether as a civil servant or as a member of the legal profession or of the judiciary, a political speaker or a pulpit orator, should not waste too much time, in his adolescence, on those subjects which are taught by abstract geometry. Let him, instead, cultivate his mind with an ingenious method; let him study topics, and defend both sides of a controversy, be it on nature, man, or politics, in a freer and brighter style of expression. Let him not spurn reasons that wear a semblance of probability and verisimilitude. Let our efforts not be directed towards achieving superiority over the Ancients merely in the field of science, while they surpass us in wisdom; let us not be merely more exact and more true than the Ancients, while allowing them to be more eloquent than we are; let us equal the Ancients in the fields of wisdom and eloquence as we excel them in the domain of science.

VIII

I have thus far said nothing about poetry, because poetical genius is a gift from heaven, and there exists no instrument by which it can be attained. I think however that a few words about poetry will not be amiss at this point. This excursus may perhaps be extraneous to the symmetry of my discourse, but, if you examine closely, it is not entirely outside its framework. Writers who are endowed with the poetical afflatus should, if they intend to enrich their poetry with cultural studies, select the flower of each of the various disciplines.

I have stated that the type of abstract philosophical criticism prevalent in our day is detrimental to poetry, but only if imparted as a school-subject to adolescents. That type of criticism benumbs their imagination and stupefies their memory, whereas poets are endowed with surpassing imagination, and their immanent spirit is Memory, with her children, the Muses. If adolescents whose imagination and memory have been previously strengthened are taught philosophical criticism, their poetical powers, I think, would derive benefit from the process. Poets keep their eyes focused on an ideal truth, which is a universal idea, as I shall presently explain. Even the geometrical method is conducive to the contriving of poetical figments, if the writer makes an effort to preserve throughout the continuity of the plot, the identical psychological traits which he has given to his characters at the beginning of the play. This is an art of which Homer was the earliest instructor, said Aristotle. The Philosopher points out that there are certain paralogisms *a consequente,* such as: *Daedalus flies, if he has wings.* Poetic figments cannot be handled in the correct fashion except by artists who can link properly point to point, so that the second point seems to proceed naturally from the first, and the third from the second. It was acutely but truthfully said that figments of this kind can be invented only by persons intimately familiar with philosophic truths. This is done outstandingly by geometricians who, working from hypothetical or incorrect premises and data, are able to deduce conclusions which are true.

I believe that the goal which today is most particularly pursued, i.e., ideal or universal truth, is exceedingly serviceable to poetry. By no means do I share the opinion that poets take special delight in falsehoods. I would even dare to affirm that poets are no less eager in the pursuit of truth than philosophers. The poet teaches by delighting what the philosopher teaches austerely. Both teach moral duties; both depict human habits and behavior; both incite to virtue and deter from vice. But the philosopher, addressing himself to cultivated men, treats these matters in a generic way. The poet, instead, because his business is with the majority of men, induces persuasion by giving plastic portrayals of exalted actions and characters; he works, as it were, with "invented" examples. As a result, he may depart from the daily semblances of truth, in order to be able to frame a loftier semblance of reality. He departs from inconstant, unpredictable nature in order to pursue a more constant, more abiding reality. He creates imaginary figments which, in a way, are more real than physical reality itself.

The inflexibility of human behavior, the rigor of moral conscience, i.e., the duty of the individual person to be, in all of his doings and under all circumstances, consistent with himself, was excellently inculcated by the Stoics, of whom, in my opinion, modern philosophers are the exact counterpart. The Stoics were quite right in claiming that Homer had been the earliest exponent of their doctrines, if we consider that, in Aristotle's view, Homer was the most outstanding inventor of poetical figments. And I think that the same reasons which prompted me to judge that the trend of our studies is detrimental to the prudent conduct of interpersonal relationships apply in support of the claim that that trend is, instead, beneficial to poetry.

Practical judgment in human affairs seeks out the truth as it is, although truth may be deeply hidden under imprudence, ignorance, whim, fatality, or chance; whereas poetry focuses her gaze on truth as it ought to be by nature and reason.

Modern physics too, I would be inclined to think, is conducive to the poetic craft. Poets, today, employ expressions describing the natural causes of physical phenomena, either because they wish to arouse our admiration for the brilliance of their diction, or because they intend to vindicate their ancient

claim, the earliest poets having been singers of physical phenomena. Notice such expressions as "blood-sprung" for "be-
gotten," "to vanish into the air" for "to die," "breast-burning
fire" for "fever," "air-condensed vapor" for "cloud," "cloud-
flung fire" for "thunderbolt," "earth-shadows," for "night."
In ancient times, all the subdivisions of time were expressed
in terms of the astronomers; poetic diction abounded in me-
tonymy, by which the cause, instead of the effect, is stated. In
conclusion, inasmuch as modern physics borrows its most
sensuous images, expressive of natural causes, from mechanics,
which it uses as its instrument, it endows poets with a treasure
of new expressions both striking and novel.

IX

Perhaps you may have been wondering why, in speaking of the instruments by which knowledge is procured, I
made no mention of Christian theology. But I trusted that you
would not expect me to draw an indecorous comparison between truth and falsehood, between divine and human things,
between Christ on one side, and Lycurgus or Numa on the
other.[27] But to understand the serious errors committed by
the thinkers of paganism in theology, note, in the first place,
that they entertained a multitude of contradictory and vague
opinions as to the nature of the gods; secondly, that the rulers
of the pagan world tolerantly allowed philosophers to profess
antithetical opinions on divine things, and that they penalized
the impiety only of such thinkers as denied the existence of
the gods. This tolerance was prompted, perhaps, by the
thought that the ideas voiced by philosophers went far above

[27] According to an ancient tradition, which modern research has undermined (but some scholars still cling to its historicity), Lycurgus was the
author of the constitution of Sparta (*ca.* 880 B.C.). The Spartan legislation
seems to stem from Crete, where Lycurgus is said to have died. Numa
Pompilius was the second king of Rome. According to a remote legend,
he is said to have established the main religious and ritual institutions of
Rome.

the heads of the multitude, in whom it was necessary to inculcate religion. Poets were likewise permitted, in order to render their mythological figments more attractive, to invent all sorts of singular notions concerning the gods and their powers; for these notions were felt as conducive to religion, in that the masses were imbued with a more grandiose opinion of the might of their deities. In regard to sacrifices and to the taking of omens and auspices, the rulers insisted on the preservation of the most exact ritualism and of the strictest solemnities. [It was in these manifestations that the august and venerable character, the awesome prestige of religious pageants and rites principally consisted.] Hence, penalties and protective measures were attached only to the pollution of ceremonies, to contempt for the rites of the auspices or to the introduction of new forms of divination. Christians were persecuted not because the votaries of Christ had no belief in pagan gods, but because they refused to participate in the public worship. But what could be more foolish and inept than to prescribe absolutely fixed ceremonies for the vague, shifting deities of Paganism? Christianity, instead, advocates unassailable dogmas bearing on the nature of God and on the mysteries of religion; hence the exactness of its rituals is fully justified.

A new discipline has providentially arisen among us for the disclosure of the divine sources of Truth as well as for the illustration and interpretation of the sacred books and traditions; it is called dogmatic theology. In antiquity, the Law of the Twelve Tables began with a chapter concerning ritual observances, *Deos caste adeunto* ["let purity guide our approach to the gods"]; the Code of Justinian, instead, opens with the title, "Concerning the most high Trinity and Catholic faith."

Another branch of religious studies, moral theology, stems from, and uses the excellent method of, dogmatic theology. Moral theology expounds the precepts of the good, and the virtues and duties which are in harmony with the Christian religion. This science of God, this purity of ceremonies, these doctrines of morality are characterized by such truth, intrinsic dignity, and moral power, that the propagation of Christianity was not due, like that of other world faiths, to the might of arms and the obliteration of whole nations; it was brought about, instead, by the virtues of its martyrs, and the constancy with which they withstood the tortures inflicted on them. It was among two of the most cultured nations of antiquity that Christianity spread, and became a part of the most powerful empire on earth. These peoples, one with its empire, the other with its learning, spontaneously yielded to Christianity; and it was doubtless by a divine dispensation that the monuments of pagan religion and knowledge were not annihilated. Throughout the length of time, whenever Christianity and paganism are compared, heathenism is seen to be human, Christianity altogether divine.

X

Hitherto the instruments of knowledge have been discussed. Let us examine the complementary aids to our study methods.

The systematization in preceptive form of many subjects that depend on common sense does harm rather than benefit to our study methods. In those subjects in which discretion and practical common sense are supreme, a great number of preceptive treatments is no more helpful than their absence.

In the first place, efforts which are directed to the preceptive arrangement of the criteria of discretion are unprofitable. Discretion takes guidance from the countless particularities of events; as a consequence any attempt to grasp those detailed aspects, no matter how inclusive, is always insufficient.

In the second place, such preceptive treatments foster a habit of abiding by general maxims; in real life, nothing is more useless. In the disciplines that depend on sound judgment (oratory, poetics, art of history-writing), let us regard such preceptive aids merely as *dei compitales*, i.e., merely as road signs, indicating in what direction and by what path the student should walk. He should walk, needless to say, in the direction of philosophy, toward the contemplation of the ideal patterns of nature itself.

When undivided attention was given to the cultivation of philosophy, or (which is the same) when the contemplation of the "ideal nature" was kept in view, Greece, Rome, and the modern epoch experienced the greatest flowering of superior writers in each of those arts. But as soon as preceptive treatments regulating those arts were composed, the writers that arose were not similarly outstanding. Try to search for the reasons that account for these two phenomena, and you will find that I have quoted the correct one. In the past, all arts and disciplines were interconnected and rested in the lap of philosophy; subsequently, they were sundered apart. Those responsible for this separation can be compared to a tyrannical ruler who, having seized mastery of a great, populous, and opulent city, should, in order to secure his own safety, destroy the city and scatter its inhabitants into a number of widely strewn villages. As a consequence, it is impossible for the townsmen to feel inspired, through the bold pride awakened by the sight of the splendor and wealth of their city and by the awareness of their number, to band together and conspire against him, lending one another help in their fight against the common oppressor.

XI

The validity of the preceding remarks is borne out by our contemporary way of studying and practicing law. Since legal science as a discipline was unknown among the Greeks, and the Romans had an entirely different conception of it, some principles which are inherent in this topic and have reference to my theme may be discussed here.

The first four titles of Book I of Justinian's Pandects, relating to matters which the Byzantine jurists call *"Ta Prota"* (First Principles), i.e., those sections which expound the doctrine concerning the nature of legal theory, its aim (justice), its subject matter (law), the causes and specific features of legal enactments, and the manner of interpreting them, occupy but a small part of that great work. Yet the whole "art of the law" is contained in those sections.[28] The very designations "art of the law," "art of jurisprudence" seem to ring false. There is only one "art" of prudence, and this art is philosophy. As the learned author of the "Method of Civil Law"[29] phrases it, *Ta Prota,* or "The First Principles" contain the philosophy of law, while the rest of the *Corpus Juris* is devoted to legal history. I would subjoin that the *Corpus Juris* contains, in addition, a very large collection of legal cases, and that it constitutes the outstanding example of a treatise on the forms of judicial argument (*ars topica judicialis*).

It is interesting to speculate on the strange fact that whereas we moderns possess an immense number of books on law, as did the Romans after the promulgation of the *Edictum Perpetuum,* prior to that time the Romans had very few, and the Greeks possessed no works on law.[30] Why?

[28] The *Digesta seu Pandectae* were published in A.D. 533 and constitute Part II of the *Corpus Juris Civilis,* the famous codification (*ca.* A.D. 534), which Emperor Justinian (527–565) caused to be compiled, and which encompasses about one thousand years of Roman legal development. The Pandects are a collection of excerpts from the writings of Roman *jurisprudentes,* arranged in 50 books. The revival of the study of Roman law in twelfth-century Italy goes back to the rediscovery of the Pandects, after the long medieval "night." (On the immense influence of the *Corpus Juris* on European civilization, see the instructive volume by Paul Koschaker, *Europa und das römische Recht* [Munich: Biederstein, 1947].) The first four titles of the Pandects, which deal with the definition of the basic principles of legal science, are entitled respectively: I. *De justitia et jure;* II. *De Origine juris et omnium magistratuum et successione prudentum;* III. *De legibus senatusque consultis et longa consuetudine;* and IV. *De Constitutionibus principum.* Nicolini thinks that when the Byzantine jurists spoke of *Ta Prota,* they actually were alluding, not to the first four *titles* of Book I of the Pandects, but to the first four *books* of that work.

[29] The author of this manual (which Corsano is unable to identify) is probably either Hermannus Vultejus or Nicholaus Vigel. See, under these names, Stintzing-Landsberg, *Geschichte der deutschen Rechtswissenschaft.*

[30] "Through the *Edictum Perpetuum,* issued in A.D. 121 by Salvius Julianus, by order of Emperor Hadrian, the publication of the *Edictum*

The reason is that in Greece the task of teaching the philosophy of law, that is, the theory of the state, of justice, and of laws, devolved on the philosophers. The so-called *"pragmatics,"* i.e., the "sheer practitioners," supplied legislative material to the orators; the function of pleading cases, and of devising arguments in equity from the actual facts, fell almost exclusively to the orators. In other words, the legal profession, in Greece, had three aspects: (1) the philosophers' knowledge of theory, (2) the *pragmatics'* conversancy with positive legislation and its history, (3) the orators' forensic ability. The Greeks possessed countless books on philosophy, a great many eloquent speeches, but no technical books on law.

At Rome, the philosophers themselves were jurists since, in the Romans' view, the whole range and compass of knowledge was involved in legal expertise. The Roman jurists thus became the chief instruments for the preservation of the unadulterated *"sapientia"* of the "heroic epoch," since, in the words of the poet:

> In this did pristine wisdom consist:
> in the separation of public from private rights,
> of sacred from profane matters,
> in the prevention of marriages forbidden by law,
> in fixing the rights of husbands,
> establishing urban communities,
> carving laws on wooden tablets.
>
> [Horace, *Ars poetica* 396–399]

Notice that the same definition served the Romans for jurisprudence and the Greeks for wisdom: "the knowledge of things divine and human." And since, in Rome, *sapientia* corresponded perfectly to justice and statesmanship, the Romans were in a better position than the Greeks to master the art of government and of justice, not by talking about it, but by direct experience in public affairs. Thus, following "a real,

---

Praetoris (which year after year, brought private Roman Law up to date) was discontinued, and the first attempt was made at a reorganization (not a codification) of the already very copious juridical materials" (Corsano). See A. Guarino, *Salvius Julianus* (1946).

not a counterfeit philosophy" (these words of the jurist still seem apposite when applied to Rome's primitive, "heroic" epoch) the Romans first strengthened themselves in their inclination to law by scrupulously taking on public duties, serving as magistrates, as military commanders; and at a later time, in their old age, after having mastered the practical virtues, turned their minds toward law as the most highly esteemed and dignified employment of their old age.

The patricians, however, made use of their knowledge of the law as of an *arcanum,* a secret source of power. In Rome, the body politic consisted of only three social classes: plebeians, knights, senators. The patricians did not constitute a class apart and we would have no reliable account of them if they had not, by some scheme, raised for themselves a ladder of power in the republic. Law was of three kinds: sacral, including the law of the auspices; public law, embracing the law of embassy; and private, covering the *formulae* of judicial proceeding. The patricians, craving to obtain an influence, if not entire at least partial, over the assemblies of the people (*comitia*), which could be held only when the auspices were favorable and which took up matters relating to war, peace, alliances, and public justice, bethought themselves of the device: that no one should be considered a jurist unless he knew all three kinds of law. Hence, their definition of the art of law as "a knowledge of divine and human affairs."

But no one knew all of the three branches of law, except the members of the *collegia* of the *pontifices* or augurs; and inasmuch as none but noblemen could be members of those *collegia,* the patricians alone guarded jurisprudence, as some kind of mystery. After the time of Tiberius Coruncanius,[31] who was the first to profess law in Rome, the art of law, as if

---

[31] "Tiberius Coruncanius, third century B.C., the first *pontifex maximus* of plebeian stock (according to Pomponius, in *Digesta,* I, 2, 2, 38) was the first to violate the pontifical secret concerning the *formulae juris,* by having them recited in public" (Corsano). See H. F. Jolowicz, *Historical Introduction to the Study of Roman Law* (Cambridge, Eng.: University Press, 1932); also Adolf Berger, *Encyclopedic Dictionary of Roman Law* (Philadelphia: American Philosophical Society, 1953).

something holy, was taught exclusively to the sons of the most aristocratic families. In order to render this secret of their power more impressive through the sacred aura that surrounded the laws, the patricians religiously guarded the text of the laws; and in order to bestow on legal enactments a still more venerable prestige, they saw to it that the *formulae* of judicial proceedings should be absolutely fixed and endowed with the utmost solemnity. Furthermore, in order to keep the mysteries of the law hidden as much as possible from the plebeians, they abridged the enactments instead of writing them out in full.

Here it must be observed that in preserving the secret for themselves the Romans proved their wisdom. There was justification for their belief that the aristocracy, whose capacity for war-making was necessary to the community, could accomplish more by the pursuit of strict justice than by acts of injustice and overbearing insolence. The aura of secrecy surrounding justice, moreover, aroused in the people the greatest reverence for law.

That body politic is most fortunate, indeed, where the rigorous observance of the law binds citizens together like the worship of an unknown god; where communal discipline is maintained with no less impartiality and firmness than in an army, where no soldier is allowed to question an order, his only duty being to await commands alertly and execute them.

Hence law in the free republic of Rome was extremely rigid and inflexible; the praetor was merely the "keeper of the civil law"; all contracts were affirmed by "solemn stipulations"; all transfers of sums of money, either on occasion of a promise of payment, or of the actual discharging of a debt, were made at the bankers' tables, on signature. If judicial remedies were lacking, the cases were contested in the courtroom, and the controversy was decided on the basis of the depositions of the parties concerning the "formal promises" (*sponsiones*) that had previously occurred. If good men wanted to deal in good faith with other good men, they did not bring suit before the judges, but tried to reach an agreement through arbitral decision, where the controlling factor was not the inflexible unchangeableness of the law but considerations of moral duty. As for individuals who appeared to deserve exemption from the law for merit, or required unprecedented penalties for crime, the provisions of the Law of the Twelve Tables (which Tacitus rightly, and I suppose for this reason, calls *finem aequi juris,* the ultimate in equitable law) were not slackened or made more rigorous; but extraordinary enactments, *"privilegia,"* were issued. Only urgent and immediate issues made it necessary to take measures entirely outside the ordinary course of justice.

Thus, the law was uniformly unbending. If, at times, necessity to protect the common welfare, and, at times, private utility, dictated the introduction of some new rules infringing on the law, the jurists resorted to legal fictions and excogitated some formal devices of their own invention so as to avoid amending the law. Examples of fictions were the *post-liminium,* the fiction of the *Lex Cornelia,* and others, such as the imaginary sales which were supposed to take place in the emancipation of minors and in will-making.

On close inspection, it will be found that legal fictions are nothing but extensions of, and exceptions to, the rulings of ancient Roman law; it was by means of such fictions that the jurists succeeded in adjusting facts to law. Today, instead, our practice is to adjust law to facts. Ancient jurisprudence became famous for such ingenious devices, through which laws were kept inviolate and public need was provided for.

The patricians, then, were the only ones entitled to exercise the profession of law. Forensic oratory, however, could be engaged in by new men as well as by those of obscure birth. The Roman jurists were learned in the philosophy and history of the law, and, even when they did not undertake to plead cases in court, they gave legal opinions to the clients who came to consult them. These opinions were passed on to the orators like oracular responses. When the jurists themselves went to the Forum to plead, it was in cases in which legal points were involved. The literal wording of the text of a

legal instrument concerns law, but the intention embodied in
that instrument belongs to equity. Legitimate cases rest on
both written documents and their intent. Each acting in accordance with his profession, the jurist based his defense on the
letter of the law and the great orator on equity. Since a supreme, almost sacred inviolability was attached to the law, it
was not possible to obtain from the judges an equitable sentence unless by the employment of exceptional eloquence.

And for these reasons, in the free republic of Rome, there
existed three subdivisions of the law, but one single art of
law, or jurisprudence, which was termed a "knowledge of
divine and human affairs, the science of justice and injustice."
In this definition, "human affairs" include affairs both public
and private, while the word "justice" was understood to cover
whatever had been explicitly provided for by the law. Jurisprudence and forensic oratory were, by deliberate intent of
the Republic, separate; whenever the jurists exercised oratory
they strictly adhered to the letter of the legal provision; the
orators abided sometimes by the words, sometimes by the spirit
of the law; and, while even mediocre orators could invoke the
letter, only the most eloquent could vindicate the spirit of
the law. There was but a small number of law books and not
a single one of them, unless by stealth, was available to the
public. But when the Republic underwent a transformation
and became a principate, the rulers of Rome, who at the
beginning had transferred the right of summoning the assemblies of the people (*comitia*) from the people to the Senate,
soon arrogated to themselves the absolute right to the totality
of state decisions involving war, peace, alliances, as well as
other matters of high policy. The *arcana* of military and
political power were locked up in the secrecy of the ruler's
palace. Crispus used to tell Livia that "the account is accu-
rately kept and proves right only if rendered to a single person";[32] this saying reveals that the *lex regia*, to which the

32 Sallustius Crispus was a nephew of the historian Gaius Sallustius
Crispus, the first Roman historian presenting highly artistic and literary
qualities as a writer. Livia was the wife of Augustus. Crispus' phrase cogently characterizes the moment when, as Ruvo says, "authority shifts

jurists allude, and through which the people were supposed to have transferred their sovereignty to the Emperor, was not voted spontaneously, but was brought about by an inescapable emergency of the Republic. Under the stress of that emergency, Augustus, under the name of princeps, "assumed the supreme power of a state torn by fratricidal strife." He proceeded to govern with a truly sovereign hand.

But with a view to giving some measure of satisfaction to the aristocratic class and to the Senate, the Roman Emperors, mindful of the fact that the optimates had opposed the stabilization of the principate, granted them these semblances of power. The Senate was allowed to issue enactments covering matters of private law; not, however, on its own initiative, but in accord with previous proposals by the Emperor. These imperial proposals, or law bills, were couched in the form of "reports" by the *consules;* but in reality were personal decisions by the Emperor on which the Senate had the privilege of voting. Consequently, the Senate had no power to issue any legal enactment on any private matter, except that, on subjects agreeable to him, the ruler permitted the Senate to vote in the manner which he desired.

While imperial dominance was being strengthened, it was the Emperor himself who read those consular "reports"; while after the consolidation of his rule, the Emperor spoke through specially appointed questors. The right of publicly giving decisions having legal force—*jus respondendi*—was granted by the Emperors; however, not indiscriminately, not to any nobleman, but only to individuals of unquestioned devotion. To the *jus respondendi* was attached an authority seemingly greater than that which that privilege had carried at any previous time. But the decisions of the jurists had legal force only for the case on which they were consulted. Furthermore, in order to undermine even this mere semblance of aristocratic power, and to strengthen their own actual rule through the devotion of the masses and the favor of the crowd, the Emperors allowed

from the free patricians, representing the Republic, to the Emperor, who levels under his rule patricians, knights, and plebeians."

the praetors to mitigate the inflexibility of the law by an equitable interpretation whenever the law bore too heavily upon private individuals. As a consequence, where it was inapplicable, praetors could stretch it favorably.

In the absence of a law, the praetor was instructed to fill up the void by a benignant sentence. Never could the praetor change the existing provisions outright, but with a semblance of fidelity to the established legal provisions, he could invalidate their force and nullify existing rules by resort to interpretative fiction—just as was done by the jurist of the free republican period. This was done, for instance, in cases of *bonorum possessio,* or in proceedings involving the rescission of contracts.

Thus the praetors became, at the same time, the preservers of the established legal system and the promoters of natural equity. If the literal wording of the law bore squarely upon the case, their practice was to apply specific actions; when a legal text was equivocal or inapplicable, they granted actions in equity.

Thus under the principate, but even previous to the enactment of the *Edictum Perpetuum,* jurisprudence had already changed, since the expression "human affairs" (*humanae res*) designated private questions only; and public law was separate from private. As a consequence, legal philosophy began to decline.

It was still a "science of justice," but by gradual steps, it was being ousted by praetorian *aequitas.* Legal books were still few in number, since jurists still professed to adhere to the strict letter of the law, still clung to precedent, and only the orators undertook to plead the equitable side of cases.

Then, under Hadrian, the *Edictum Perpetuum* was published as the grand repository of *aequitas;* and a public order was issued that, where the study of law had previously begun with the Twelve Tables, now such a study should have its starting point in the *Edictum Perpetuum.* The Law of the Twelve Tables ceased to be looked upon as the basic source of Roman law.[33] The law-creating powers, granted to Senate, praetors, and jurists was enfeebled. The decisions of the Senate were no longer conformable to the provisions of the Twelve Tables, nor did the praetors henceforward pattern on them the rules which they issued for the duration of their office (the so-called *edicta perpetuae jurisdictionis*). Imperial rescripts, infused with natural equity, set about creating new norms, and promulgated solutions for doubtful legal cases, Therefore, the chronology of the imperial enactments—*constitutiones*—begins with Hadrian. Jurisprudence was transformed from the science of the just into an art of equity, a technique of the equitable. The jurists strove to find points of equity in litigation, and began compiling a number of books on private law. As the procedural *formulae* were still operative, the orators, in the courts, still turned to the defense of the equitable. However, as natural *aequitas* became prevalent, forensic oratory fell into silence.

Later, when Constantine abolished the "formulary" system of judicial actions and ordered all cases to follow the so-called *extra ordinem* procedure, the mysteries of law were unveiled to all, and law, which had been a tool of power in the hands of the patricians, was wrested from their grasp. Persons of humble origin were allowed to engage in the profession of law. Public institutions devoted to law-teaching were founded in Rome, Constantinople, Beirut; and finally, in the interest of the state, Theodosius II and Valentinian IV issued a decree ordering that no person, not even a public law-professor, should teach law in private.[34]

[33] The Law of the Twelve Tables, covering all areas of Roman law, was drawn up by a special commission, *Decemviri legibus scribundis*, in 451–450 B.C. It was the earliest Roman code of laws, and marks the beginning of Roman juridical growth.

[34] "That is, Theodosius II prescribed that professors in the public schools of Constantinople could not simultaneously engage in private instruction" (Nicolini). Nicolini gives the reference to *Codex Theodosianus* I. 3. 3. Theodosius II lived from A.D. 401 to 450 and ruled from 408 to 450. The publication of the *Codex Theodosianus* (438) was his most notable achievement.

Whenever equity suggested a more lenient interpretation, the rules of the *jus civile* were set aside, not with overanxious formalities, and by means of ingenious fictional contrivances, but openly; and not only by the emperors but by the judges as well. *Aequitas* began to be the controlling factor of all controversies in the courtroom; the praetor, the "living voice of the *jus civile*," began to be the unchallenged arbiter of all private law, as is any of our judges today. Where, once, there were many judgments and few arbitral verdicts (since there are many lawbreakers and few equitable men), today, instead, the practice of arbitration prevails, and equity has been transformed into a necessary feature of our positive law.

It may be added that, when Constantine was converted to Christianity (in which the knowledge of divine affairs is found in the Fathers of the Church), jurisprudence concerned itself only with purely private matters, and was no longer a "science of justice." The modern jurist is no longer tied to a scrupulous compliance with the letter of the law. Since natural equity rules our courtrooms, forensic oratory has fallen mute. Our law groans under the great bulk of its books. With both apt expressiveness and truth, one may say that in actual litigation the modern jurist has encroached upon the province of the orator; while, in fictitious legal controversies, he has usurped the role of the rhetorician.

Jacques Cujas frankly admits that whenever he did not have an authentic legal case to deal with, he took up the scholastic debates of the rhetoricians.[35] The author, whoever he is, of the celebrated essay "On the Causes of the Corruption

[35] Jacques Cujas (1522–1590) was the brightest star in the galaxy of French humanistic scholars who carried on the traditions of the school founded by Andrea Alciati. Cujas taught at Bourges, 1575–1590. He applied his immense mastery of classical philology, *antiquitates* (archaeology), institutional, political, and social history, to the reconstruction of Roman law. Cujas' interest was mainly directed at textual exegesis and at the identification of the juristic individuality and the doctrinal contributions of single Roman *jurisprudentes*. Cujas' researches stood in contrast with the theoretico-conceptual-systematic trend represented by Hugues Doneau (Donellus), 1527–1591.

of Eloquence," failed to include in his catalogue this source of oratorical decline; perhaps because the decay had barely begun to arise in his time, and it is very hard to notice the moment when an evil appears; usually, that moment escapes the attention of even the keenest and most foresighted observer.

Let us now go back to our discussion of the transformation of Roman jurisprudence. Inflexible at first, rigorous observance of textual verbalism was the *arcanum,* the secret, of patrician power against the plebeians; subsequently, having been liberalized, it was the secret of imperial power against the patricians. During the free republican period, it was essential to the common interest that the science of law should not become public property; during the imperial age, it was a vital concern to the emperors that it should *not* remain concealed. Formerly all men in Rome were familiar with public law, but private law was kept secret; later, public law became an *arcanum,* while private law was divulged to all. Once, the student learned public law first and private law at a subsequent time; today, those persons who are versed in private law proceed to deliberations of state. In the past, the science of the triple law was a unity; today it is divided into three branches, ecclesiastic, public, and private. Formerly, the science of private law dealt with general concepts: today it is concerned to a much greater extent with specific cases. Formerly, laws contained general provisions concerning affairs of frequent occurrence; today, legal enactments are made to cover the most circumstantially detailed factual matters. Once, there were very few laws and innumerable *privilegia;* today, the laws are so specific and numerous as to resemble so many *privilegia.* In the past, *jurisprudentia* was properly the science of formal justice; today it is, instead, the art of the equitable. Formerly, legal knowledge was universal, and characterized by inflexibility: today it is particular and pliant. Science is rigorous and unbending, whereas art is supple and adjustable to human habits and customs. In the past, the facts of "equitable" cases ran counter to formal legality, i.e., conflicted with the textual wording of the law, unless adjusted to it by an interpretation based on fictions. Today, strictly legal provisions may be unequitable unless by benevolent interpretation, by a mitigating exegesis, they are accommodated to the facts. Once it was the glory of jurisprudence to apply fictions in order to square acts of equity with the law; today it is that, through liberal interpretations, just laws measure up to the facts. It was formerly traditional, among the jurists, not to depart from the strict letter of the law; today it is to the spirit of the law that they constantly resort. In legal questions, jurists formerly clung to the literal wording, orators emphasized the spirit and the intent of the law; in our day, the jurist takes over the function of the orator. Since laws are few and well-defined, while facts are infinite, and law refers to statutes while facts concern equity, law books, which in the past were exceedingly few, today have become numerous beyond counting.

In conclusion, at the time when the secrecy which surrounded the art and practice of law altered with the Roman state, laws and legal theory underwent change; the roles of jurists, orators, magistrates and law courts became quite different from what they had been. And thus we came to possess a new art of law and a new type of legal literature, and we have grown beyond the Greeks and the early Romans.

It is strange that this secret history of the *jurisprudentia* of Rome should have escaped the attention of Arnold Clapmar, the author of a volume entitled "The Secrets of Statecraft," since he was such a sagacious observer of analogous phenomena which characterized the Roman state.[36]

The foregoing remarks concerning the art of law in Antiq-

---

[36] Reference is to the *De Arcanis rerum publicarum* by Arnold Clapmar (1574–1664), Professor of Public Law at Altdorf. The *De Arcanis* is a typical expression of the political thought of the Baroque age (see V. Titone, *La politica deletà barocca* [Caltanissetta: S. Sciascia, 1950]). It is not a treatise on the *coups d'état*, but a series of portrayals of the various epochs of the history of Rome, accompanied by observations. The work was reprinted various times during the seventeenth century; the Amsterdam editions of it (1641 and 1644), in Elzevir form, are highly prized.

uity shed light upon and throw into visible relief the advantages and deficiencies of our modern methods of teaching and studying law.

It is an advantage for us that the theoretical and practical aspects of law have coalesced today into a single corpus, whereas among the Greeks law was partitioned between philosophers concerned with theory, *pragmatics,* whose interest was the history of law cases, and orators, concerned with the art of judicial pleading. In Rome, prior to the promulgation of the *Edictum Perpetuum,* the legal profession was divided between jurists and orators.

As a consequence, our study method excels that of the Greeks and the early Romans, inasmuch as a person experienced in handling the forms of judicial argument is endowed with a broader vision and is able to discern what legal norms support or promote his case; and has, thus, the advantage over a mere practitioner, who, like the Greek "pragmatic," is confined to empirical knowledge of the history of the cases. Moreover, men expert in jurisprudence perceive more sharply those elements of fact which help in winning a suit at law, and therefore are able to present the client's case more convincingly than a mere orator.

But this advantage of ours is offset by a drawback; modern jurisprudence is healthier because of being separated from eloquence, but weaker in its separation from philosophy. In our day, legal practitioners are not apt to win a case by a dramatic speech, as the orators of antiquity often did. On the other hand, our lawyers are deficient in the knowledge of how to set in order and maintain a commonwealth through laws; this knowledge, as the source of all jurisprudence, should be taught first, but is not taught as the philosophers used to teach it, and as the Romans mastered it, by practical experience in the discharge of governmental duties.

It is a clear advantage for us that, today, we do not need much eloquence to gain equitable adjudications of legal disputes. In the courtroom it is indeed sufficient to discover a straightforward presentation of the arguments in equity, based on a close examination of the facts, so that the law may easily be adjusted to such facts by taking into consideration, not its verbal formulation, but its spirit. In antiquity, instead, the intervention of Marcus Crassus, a consummate orator, was required to champion the cause of equity and defend the will of the dead in the case of Marcus Curius *vs.* Mucius Scaevola, where Scaevola stood firmly on the literal interpretation of the law.[37] Today any peasant, however halting and ineloquent, would be able to obtain justice by demonstrating the equitable points in his plea. But the sanctity of the law is diminished; for he who seeks exemption from a law brands that enactment as faulty, charges the legislator with imprudence, and impairs the prestige of the law. We all know that a law undermined by shortcomings and by exceptions brought up against it, may never have a chance fully to reassert its former prestige.

Mention should be made here of a wise expedient which was resorted to by Agesilaus of Sparta. He had introduced a law by which draft-dodgers were to be severely punished. There was a great scarcity of soldiers, and Agesilaus was anxious to spare the youths, the flower and strength of the Spartan state. Without issuing a new law and in order that the authority of the law which condemned them should not be impaired, he ordered that the law should go into effect on the day following the trial of the draft-dodging youths. This scheme devised by the King of Sparta has striking parallels in some of the Roman legal fictions.

A further advantage of our system is that our law experts aim more at equity than at strict law and treat private individuals with greater consideration. The ancient Romans, instead, were very strict in complying with the law, and this

[37] "Quintus Mucius Scaevola (born 140 B.C.) was pontifex, quaestor, tribune of the people, praetor, and consul (95 B.C.). Jointly with L. Licinius Crassus, he promulgated the *Lex Licinia Mucia*, which by stiff limitations, hampered the acquisition of Roman citizenship on the part of the *Latini:* this contributed to the outbreak of civil war. Scaevola's successor, M. Curius, sued him at law. Scaevola's defense was pleaded by M. Crassus" (Ruvo). See Cicero, *De Oratore* I. 39; II. 32.

accrued to the good of their commonwealth. To demonstrate the inflexibility of justice in a specific case instills in all citizens a deeper reverence for the law. On the occasion of the interchange of prisoners between Carthage and Rome, the most serious grounds of equity were in favor of the release of all Carthaginian prisoners in order to obtain the liberation of Regulus.[38] Yet in his desire that there be no exception to the law, he took the decision for which he is renowned—to return to Carthage. That was an undying example of faith toward the enemy, loyalty to his country and of unmatched firmness of soul, expressed in imperishable wisdom.

Today our proceeding from the study of private to that of public law is undoubtedly an advantage. Before being entrusted with state matters, we receive training in affairs in which failure would result in least damage to the state. But in early Rome, where the public safety was the supreme law, and the common good was the matrix of all equity, training in public law was obtained in the discharge of magistracies and military commands, and then private law could be taken up.

We must, finally, count as an advantage the fact that the professions of legal expert and orator are, in our age, joined in the same person, even in cases where factual matters are predominant. In early Rome, jurist and orator were distinct. Consequently, in cases of fact, the modern lawyer can be more authoritative, whereas in those of law he can be more eloquent. But this advantage is offset by the fact that the science of threefold law, once unitary, has today been dismembered into three distinct disciplines: ecclesiastical (or canon) law, public, and

[38] Marcus Atilius Regulus, Roman consul in the First Punic War. Was captured by the enemy army in 255. B.C. and during peace negotiations was sent as a hostage to Rome, in the expectation that he would advise his compatriots to accept the conditions set by Carthage. Instead, he urged rejection of those conditions. On returning to Africa, he was put to death by cruel torture. Regulus is the protagonist of a famous play by Metastasio (Pietro Trapassi, 1698–1782), the greatest writer of opera librettos of the *Settecento*.

private law. Ecclesiastical and private law which, in the past, were offshoots of public law, are now severed both from public law and from each other. Canon law is the exclusive realm of theologians and ecclesiastics; members of the governmental councils monopolize public law; jurists devote their time to private law only.

I do not know whether the following drawback is compensated for by any advantage. Since equity is tested by facts, and facts are countless, containing often a multitude of points of very little importance, we have, as a result, an unbounded number of legal rules, dealing, for the most part, with extremely picayune and trifling questions. Being innumerable, such rules cannot all be complied with, and those dealing with unimportant matters easily fall into contempt, and detract from the ascendancy of momentous ones. In this connection Alfonso, King of the Congo, into whose hands a ponderous volume of Portuguese laws had fallen, although a barbarian, scoffed at their pedantic meticulousness, and inquired of some Portuguese travelers who happened to pass through his territory, what punishment was set down for one who might have touched the ground with his foot.

The early Romans, on the other hand, had few laws, but these concerned matters of extreme importance. Such was, for instance, the Law of the Twelve Tables, the "source of all Roman law" which was contained in one thin book, and was memorized by Roman boys to form their character. In my view, that scarcity of Roman laws was not counterbalanced by the *privilegia,* or enactments on behalf of individuals. Such enactments, Tacitus gravely points out, "although sometimes issued against criminals on occasion of particular misdeeds, often sprang from the matrix of class strife, or were introduced by violence for the purpose of awarding some high appointment, of banishing into exile some prominent personality, or for some other equally wicked aim."

I reject the assumption that in Rome the great number of *privilegia* acted as a counterweight to the penury of laws. The *privilegia* were looked upon with contempt, and did not constitute precedents. But minute statutes, on the other hand, are definitely considered to constitute precedents.

We, then, enjoy the advantages which have been indicated, but have been unable to avoid the drawbacks incident to them. Let us now cast a glance at the history of Roman law studies, from the medieval period to Andrea Alciati and beyond.

Accursius (1182–1259) and his extremely keen-minded followers were industrious searchers for the grounds of equity, and judiciously interpreted Roman law, adjusting it to the conditions of their time. From this viewpoint, the labors of Accursius and of his followers were admirable. Working on a great mass of extremely minute and, for our purposes, thoroughly unserviceable legislation, the Accursians attempted to enucleate certain general principles, indispensable in opinion-giving and in passing judgment. Their *summae legum* are generalized syntheses of private law, very cleverly and skillfully composed. Accursius and the Accursians unquestionably deserve Grotius' truthful and serious praise: "They are excellent at creative juristic work, even though they remain poor interpreters of the positive law." [39] Unlike the *decemviri* (451 B.C.), whose main effort was to fit Greek legislation to the Roman state, the Accursians attempted to adjust the laws of Rome to the conditions of modern time. But, again, the Accursians, in their commentaries on Roman texts, have devised countless special cases and have caused jurisprudence to incur the evils of a too minute preoccupation with details.

Andrea Alciati finally came and founded a school which

[39] Francesco Accursio di Bagnolo (near Florence) is a great name in the history of Italian legal science. He is the author of the celebrated *Glossa magna* (also called *Glossa ordinaria*) on the *Corpus Juris*. The "Postglossators" (Bartolo da Sassoferrato, Alberico da Rosate, Saliceto, etc.) are heavily indebted to Accursius, hence the designation "Accursians." Accursio taught at Bologna. A few years ago, Torelli took the initiative in proposing that Accursius' *Glossa* be reprinted in a national edition, and published valuable preliminary studies with a view to that publication.

the jurists of France followed with great honor.[40] As the outstanding ancient jurists were called after their masters, so
Andrea's disciples should be called Alciatians. Thanks to
their scholarship in the field of Latin and Greek and to their
profound knowledge of Roman history, they restored Roman
law to its pristine luster.

Yet actually Alciati and his school gave back to Rome her
own laws, instead of adjusting these laws to the needs of our
epoch. Therefore, in their own practice in private law, in
giving an opinion or making a decision in some dispute today, the Alciateans do not scruple to resort to the Accursians,
and to borrow arguments in support of equity from them.

Whenever new laws are framed, it is imperative that they
should be consonant with the institutions of the state to which
they are destined; and they should be interpreted and applied
with a constant view to the nature of those institutions. In
construing laws it is indispensable to consider the structure
of the polity for which and by which they were issued. In
order rightly to interpret, for instance, that *lex regia* which
was never actually issued, but was born with the Roman
principate, the jurist will need a firm grasp of the doctrine
of monarchical government. He will have to place everything
in the context and perspective of the nature and requirements
of the monarchical regime; he will have to keep in view the
aequitas civilis, i.e., the *giusta ragione di stato* (a concept with
which only theorists of the science of politics are thoroughly

40 Andrea Alciati (1492–1550), the renovator of *culta jurisprudentia*, the
highest expression of Italian juridical humanism, taught at Avignon, Bourges, Pavia, and Bologna. Vico stresses the "historical" rather than pragmatic aspect of Alciati's reform. Although mainly centering on the exe-
getical, historico-cultural aspects of Roman law, Alciati's legal technique
was by no means contemptuous or unmindful of the achievements of the
Accursians. It is however true that, as Vico states, his greatest title to
fame is that of having restored to Roman law the luster it had in ancient times by expounding that law in a Latin of impeccably pure elegance (a far cry from the "barbaric" Latin of Glossators and Postglossators), and by bringing to bear, upon the study of the *Corpus Juris,* all the
resources of humanistic history, philology, and archaeology.

familiar). *Aequitas civilis* is the same as *aequitas naturalis* but spans a still wider compass, since it is not dependent on the utilitarian motive of the promotion of the interests of private individuals but its major concern is the public weal. But the public weal is not present in, nor belongs exclusively to, particular individuals; consequently, the common sort, who are unable to see things unless these things are placed directly under their eyes, or incapable of understanding matters which do not touch them as individuals, are ignorant of it.

As for the jurist, he shall, first of all, deem best those measures of *aequitas civilis* which are not divorced from *aequitas naturalis*. He then shall consider second in importance those measures, like *usucapio*, which although they may seem, as Justinian says, "wicked defenses" (*impia praesidia*), are more conducive to the public welfare than productive of injury to private individuals. He shall subsequently assign third place to those legal measures which may be profitable to the private citizen and not detrimental to the commonwealth. Measures profitable to single citizens, but harmful to the collectivity, are offshoots of natural, not of civil equity. But those measures inflicting harm both on private citizens and on the state are not laws of a monarchic ruler but outrageous disgraces, flagrant abuses of tyrannical power. By perpetrating them, the despot tramps upon all civil and religious rights, dooming first the state, and then himself to utter ruin.

Last, I would have the jurist study the origin, the consolidation, the growth, the culmination, and the dissolution of a great polity like the Roman Empire. Let him draw a parallel between the Roman Empire and the monarchic system of our age, in order to investigate whether the same beneficial effects spring from both of them. I would have him correlate all his definitions to the nature and power of the monarchic form of government. I will have him scrutinize the cause of public utility underlying and explaining each particular group of rules of Roman law and constituting the necessary basis of it. The purpose should be to ascertain which provisions were issued for an aim profitable to private individuals, or to monarchy; to point out those not harmful, and therefore deserving of being allowed to stand, and those which, being perceived as detrimental, should be rejected.

What is justice? It is constant care for the common good. In what does the science of law consist? In the knowledge of the best government. What is law? It is an art of watching over the public interest. What is law, or "the just"? It is the useful. What is *natural* law? The private interest of each one of us. What is the law of nations? The common good of all nations. What is civil law? The good of the commonwealth. What are the sources of law and why did the law of nature originate? That man may live in any way soever. Why did *jus gentium* arise? That man might live in security and ease. What reason accounts for the establishment of civil law? The attainment of a happy and prosperous life. Which is the highest law, the standard we are to follow whenever we interpret any legal enactment? The greatness of the state, the preservation of our ruler, the glory of both.

What causes brought about the repeal of the laws *Fufia Caninia* and *Aelia Sentia*?[41] Why were the *libertas latina* and *libertas dedititia* abrogated? Why were all freedmen made Roman citizens? So that all freeborn Romans might have a feeling of greater reverence for their emperor. Why was the cruelty of the masters toward their slaves curbed by law? In order that the slaves might be prevented from rising in revolt and jeopardizing their ruler's power. Why were the *filiifamilias* allowed by the patrimonial law to hold personal

41 The *Lex Fufia Caninia* was sponsored by the consuls L. Caninius Gallus and C. Fufidius Geminus in A.D. 2. It limited the freedom of slave manumissions by testament. This freedom was later restored to its pristine entirety by Justinian. See Gatti, "La vera data della legge Fufia Caninia," *Bullettino dell'Istituto di diritto romano* (1906), pp. 115–117.

The *Lex Aelia Sentia*, A.D. 4, was sponsored by the consuls Sextus Aelius Cato and Caius Sentius Saturninus, and concerned manumission and the legal status of manumitted slaves. Both laws, *Fufia Caninia* and *Aelia Sentia*, were issued by decision of Augustus. Ruvo says that "the abolition of these laws, which took place during the epoch of the absolutistic Principate, was equivalent to the intention of enlisting for the monarchic cause the favor of the masses."

property? In order that it might be possible to impose fines on them and to deter them from criminal acts. Why were legitimations established? To mitigate the harshness of the patricians. Why are the *dominium ex jure Quiritium* and the *jus bonorum,* the *usucapio* in Italy and the *possessio longi temporis* in the provinces, institutions which in the past were distinct, now united? Why were all the subjects of the Roman Empire granted citizenship? Was it perhaps in order that the *arcanum* might be still more deeply respected, since there was a chance that the emperor might be chosen out of the provinces? Or perhaps—and this seems to be closer to the truth—so that all should have equal interest in the preservation of the Roman Empire? Why was it prescribed by law that all donations should be made public? So that no one could stir up trouble by secretly bribing the people. Why were the privileges of the soldiers extended? So that they might be more eager to support the power of their ruler. Why did the performance of trust-entails, which were formerly left entirely to the personal responsibility of the individuals who had to carry them out, subsequently become an obligation enforced by law? In order that the allies of Rome, formerly excluded from the right to inherit Roman property, should be permitted to enjoy such a right, and should rejoice to be subjects of a Roman emperor. Why, in the law of inheritance, was the distinction between *agnati,* blood relations in the paternal line, and *cognati,* blood relations generally, abolished? In order that some individuals, drunk with the pride of an ancestral and long-continued possession of power and riches, should not become too wildly arrogant. Why were penalties made harsher? Because, the ruler not being exempt from mortality, the laws need to be more watchful and endowed with stricter severity.

I have made these cursory remarks to point out the uses and advantages of this manner of studying law, not to illustrate its advantages with specific examples—which our plan does not allow—but to gather them all in a net, so to speak, and to indicate them all together.

You can see how the world of law, which was inflexible during the growth of the Republic, became mild and slack during the decline of the Empire. At the beginning of the Empire, the study and practice of law was a deliberate scheme for strengthening the rule of the *princeps;* later it became a remedy for averting its breakdown, and finally an evil by which that rule was wrecked. After the abolition of the distinction between *agnati* and *cognati,* and the extinction of the *jus gentilitatis,* the wealth of patrician families evaporated; their renown and prestige fell into a decline, their moral and physical stamina was dissolved. So many advantages being bestowed on slaves, the native stock of freeborn Romans was gradually undermined and finally corrupted. When all the subjects of the Roman Empire achieved Roman citizenship, love of country and affection for Rome were extinguished in the native citizens. Private law having assumed such great importance, and so much favor being shown to individuals, the citizens came to realize that law was nothing but their private self-advantage, and stopped taking an interest in the common welfare. Roman and provincial law became confused, the provinces were states in their own right even before conquest had invaded them; and when the bond which had so greatly contributed to the expansion of the Empire was dissolved (the allies enjoying only the profit of praise for their loyalty, while the Romans wallowed in the glory of the name and reality of power), the Empire was gradually weakened, dismembered, and finally destroyed. In this process of dissolution of the Roman power and of the decay of eloquence, the slackening of *jurisprudentia* played a prominent role.

The modern monarch, therefore, who wishes his realm to prosper, should be well-advised to have Roman laws interpreted according to *aequitas civilis.* Let him instruct judges to adjudicate disputes in this way. Let judges, moreover, use the skill of the best lawyers in uniting public interest with private cases; let them avail themselves of their oratorical powers against the lawyers of the defense so as to give precedence always to public interest over private claims; whereas, as we know, it is the effort of the lawyers to give priority to the private claims of their clients over the public interest.

Thus the state will again benefit by the conjunction of the philosophy of law, that is, civil doctrine, with juridical doctrine and theory. The gravity and hallowed dignity of the law will be enhanced. An eloquence suited to monarchic institutions will flourish, and be as superior to the eloquence now in use, as public is superior to private law in worth, significance, and importance. In order to gain victory for their clients, eloquent lawyers do their utmost toward proving that their cases have the support of public law; and having become experts in civil doctrine, they will bring the political training that they have acquired, to bear on the governance of the state itself.

In our Supreme Court at Naples, some lawsuits are decided contrary to provisions of Roman law *ex certis causis* (as the formula runs); and in that highest Assembly of this Kingdom, *aequitas civilis,* i.e., considerations of public interest, are given precedence over grounds of purely "natural" equity. But this practice is exclusively the fruit of the wisdom of individual lawyers and judges, whose services are bounded by the normal life span of all mortal beings. But were such a practice to become traditional in all law courts, as a deliberate and constantly followed policy, it would prove to be greatly beneficial.

These remarks I saw fit to bring up apropos of the possible systematization of law into an *art,* and of other questions of analogous character.

XII

A considerable number of masterpieces seem to be of very special assistance in those intellectual activities which are based on imitation. There is a saying that, if Homer had not existed, there would have been no Vergil; and without Vergil, no Tasso. Proverbially: "It is easy to add to inventions."

But on the other hand, another and greater advantage is inventive genius. The jurists have a principle, stating, "possession is nine points of the law." Thus in most cases the inventors are foremost in time and importance and have often remained alone in their eminence. What if I declared that the most outstanding masterpieces of the arts hinder rather than help students in the field? It may be surprising, but nevertheless it is true.

Those who left us masterpieces of the arts, had before their eyes no model to imitate except the best that is in nature. But those who take as models, in order to imitate them, the highest masterpieces of art—let us say, the best paintings—are usually unable to create better ones. The reason is that whatever excellence nature had to offer in each domain of art was appropriated by the artists who came first—otherwise they would not be supreme. To equal them is also impossible, since imitators are not endowed with the force of imagination of their predecessors, nor with the vivacity and abundance of their animal spirits, nor with the same nerve structure by which these spirits are led to the hand from the brain, nor with the same technical experience and facility of composition. Since imitators cannot surpass or even equal the innovators, they can only fall short of their achievement.

This truth was recognized and expressed by Titian. While he was painting in Venice, Francisco Varga, ambassador of Charles V, asked him "why he used a style of painting so *fat*, that it seemed as if his paint brushes resembled brooms." Titian replied that "each individual must, in the art which he professes, seek praise for some excellence; and the reputation of an imitator is less than insignificant." His meaning was, that since Michelangelo had reached fame by the grandeur of his style, and Raphael by his suavity, he, Titian, was resolved to pursue an entirely different course.

May I point out that our possession of the Farnese Hercules and of other masterpieces of ancient sculpture (paintings such as Protogenes' "Ialysus" and Apelles' "Venus" have not come down to us) has prevented our sculpture from reaching its consummate fruition; whereas our painting has not failed to reach the peak of perfection. If my views on this point are erroneous, can you tell me why in Greece, in Rome, and among us (I am not speaking, now, of history-writing and oratory, which alter with political vicissitudes), language, religion, and educational methods remaining the same, the great creators of poetry have always been followed by minor figures, by pedestrian imitators? It would seem almost advisable, in order to have great artists, to have the great masterpieces of art destroyed. But since this would constitute an atrocious act of barbarism, and since few of us can aspire to the crown of greatness, let us keep our masterpieces, and let them be used for the benefit of lesser minds.

Those, instead, who are endowed with surpassing genius, should put the masterworks of their art out of their sight, and strive with the greatest to appropriate the secret of nature's grandest creations.

XIII

Unquestionably the invention of typographical characters is of signal assistance to us in our studies. Printing has enabled us to obviate all the disadvantages from which the Ancients suffered, such as the enormous cost of books and the necessity to travel long distances in order to procure and examine manuscripts. And often the Ancients were denied access to such books; the owners of them were very jealous of the invidious privilege of the sole ownership of the autograph copy. Today, on the contrary, books are in great abundance and variety, available at any place whatsoever, not only to Ptolemaic kings, but also to any private individual, and at a moderate cost. I am, however, afraid that the abundance and cheapness of books may cause us to become less industrious; we may be like banqueters, who, being surfeited with gorgeous and sumptuous dinners, wave away ordinary and nourishing food and prefer to stuff themselves with elaborately prepared but less healthy repasts.

In effect, when books were written by hand, only works composed by authors of tested and well-established reputation were reproduced, since they were the only ones worth the labor spent on the task of copying them; and since the price of such works was, at times, very high, students were obliged to copy them in their own handwriting. Now, there is no better exercise than this; we meditate on the text and write without haste or interruption, calmly and with continuous order. By copying, we gain, not a perfunctory knowledge, but an intimate familiarity with the original, and we are, so to speak, transformed into the author's very self. That is why second-rate authors palled in the copying; but superior ones were held in great esteem and celebrated, to the great profit of the general public. There is, therefore, more wit than truth in Bacon's statement that in the tidal wave of the barbarians' invasions, the major writers sank to the bottom, while the lighter ones floated on the surface. In each branch of learning, instead, it is only the most outstanding authors who have reached us, by virtue of being copied by hand. If one or another was lost, it was purely by chance.

Within my memory (and I am not yet an old man) I have seen some writers gain such renown that their works were printed twelve or more times; at present they are not merely underrated, but despised. Other authors were unread and for many years utterly forgotten, until, finally, by a stroke of luck, they were revived and are now objects of the attention of the most learned. I remember eminent scholars who roundly condemned some branches of research; now they have changed their minds and are totally absorbed by the pursuit of those subjects. This phenomenon can be accounted for in several ways. Every epoch is dominated by a "spirit," a genius, of its own. Novelty, like beauty, recommends certain faults which, after fashion changes, become glaringly apparent. Writers, wishing to reap a profit from their studies, follow the trend of their time. Literature has its own sects, allegiances, and fashions; and in the republic of letters there are rulers practiced in the mystery of grasping and holding power. And students, especially the younger and most modest, are impressed by the grand names of scholarship.

Our reading, in my opinion, should be governed by the judgment of centuries; let us place our educational methods under their auspices and protection. The Ancients should be read first, since they are of proved reliability and authority. Let us take them as standards by which to gauge the quality and validity of the moderns.

XIV

As for universities, the amazing fact is that, whereas the Ancients possessed, so to speak, universities for the body, i.e., baths and athletic fields, where young men could develop their strength and agility by exercises such as racing, jumping, boxing, javelin- and discus-throwing, swimming and bathing, they never thought of establishing universities where young minds could be cultivated and strengthened.

In Greece, a single philosopher synthesized in himself a whole university. The Greek language, so fertile in potential developments that it was admirably fitted to express not only all the occurrences of common, everyday life, but the most recondite and abstruse ideas of all sciences and arts in apt terms, the beauty of which terms was commensurate with their appropriateness and felicity; the Greek genius for lawmaking, which was so exceptional that other nations came to borrow laws from Greece while Greece had no necessity to borrow from them—these fostered among the Hellenes the conviction of their immense superiority over other nations. They were wont to ask a question, acutely symptomatic of national conceit: "Art thou a Greek or a barbarian?" as if they esteemed themselves to be worth as much as half of the world, and to be the better part of it.

Things being so, since the Greeks devoted intense, undivided attention to the cultivation of philosophy, the mother, midwife, and nursling of all sciences and arts; since they did not, in the philosophical domain, rely on authority, but discussed all problems on no other merits but the intrinsic ones, each Greek philosopher was capable of achieving a mastery of all learning, both secular and religious, and it was from him alone that students learned thoroughly whatever it was necessary for them to know in the field of public affairs.

With the Romans, the case was different. Although their speech was not autochthonous but derived from other tongues, they proudly sprung all effort to prove that a Roman word derived from other languages. In the case of the words,

... which fall from Grecian well-spring, but slightly changed,
[Horace, *Ars poetica* 53]

they preferred the frivolous, erroneous, foolish interpretation, rather than admit that one of their terms had non-native origins. Although their laws had largely been borrowed from Greece, they expended great ingenuity in grafting those enactments onto their own political system, so that they seemed to spring spontaneously from their soil. In respect to both language and law, the Romans equaled the Greeks. The need for universities was felt by the Romans even less than by the Greeks, since, as I have pointed out, they thought that wisdom consisted in the art and practice of law, and learned to master it in the everyday experience of political affairs. Since the patricians kept law-lore concealed, as if it were an *arcanum* of state, far from feeling any need for universities, the Romans had no interest whatever in establishing them.

But with the transformation of republic into principate, it be·ng in the interest of the emperors that the science of law should be propagated as legal doctrine, this discipline gradually attained greater range and compass through the multitude of writers and their division into doctrinal schools. Regular institutions of teaching were recognized, and the "Academies" of Rome, Constantinople, and Beirut were founded.

Our need for universities is considerably greater. We must have a thorough knowledge of the Scriptures and, in addition, of Eastern languages and of the canons of the ecclesiastic Councils, some of which were held in Asia, some in Europe, some in Africa, in different countries and cities, from apostolic to modern times. We must familiarize ourselves with the

laws of Romans and Lombards, with feudal law, the theories
of Greeks, Latins, and Arabs, which were introduced into our
customary public law. We must guard against scribal gar-
blings, plagiarisms, forgeries, interpolations of alien hands
through which it is difficult for us to recognize the originals,
and to grasp the author's true meaning. What we need to
know is contained in so many books in languages that are
extinct, composed by authors belonging to nations long since
vanished. These books contain allusions to custom often unknown, in corrupted codices; therefore the attainment of any
science or art has become so difficult for us, that at the present
time no person can master even a single subject. This has
made the establishment of universities necessary. In these universities, all branches of knowledge are taught by a number
of scholars, each of whom is outstanding in his particular field.
But this advantage is offset by a drawback. Arts and sciences,
all of which in the past were embraced by philosophy and
animated by it with a unitary spirit, are, in our day, unnatu-
rally separated and disjointed. In antiquity, philosophers were
remarkable for their coherence; their conduct was in full accord not only with the theories they professed but with their
method of expounding them as well. Socrates, who maintained
that "he knew nothing," never brought up any subject for discussion on his own initiative, but pretended to feel a desire to
learn from the Sophists. His habit was to confine himself to
advancing a series of minute questions, from the replies to
which he drew his own inferences. The Stoics, instead, whose
main principle was that the mind is the standard of all things,
and that the sage should not entertain "mere opinions" about
anything, established, in conformity with their requirements,
a number of unquestionable truths, linking them, by continuous concatenation, through secondary propositions, to doubtful conclusions; and employed as their instrument of argumentation the figure of the *sorites*. Aristotle, who thought
that in the attainment of truth the senses and the mind
should co-operate, made use of the syllogism, by which he
posited some universal propositions, so as to be able, in con-

crete cases, to eliminate dubiousness and to reach truth. Epi-
curus, for whom sense perception was the only avenue of approach to knowledge, neither granted any proposition to his
opponents, nor allowed them to grant any to him, but explained phenomena in the simplest and most unadorned language.

Today, students who may be trained in the art of discourse
by an Aristotelian, are taught physics by an Epicurean, metaphysics by a Cartesian. They may learn the theory of medicine from a Galenist, its practice from a chemist; they may
receive instruction in the Institutes of Justinian from a disciple of Accursius, be trained in the Pandects by a follower of
Antoine Favre,[42] in the *Codex* by a pupil of Alciati. Students'
education is so warped and perverted as a consequence, that,
although they may become extremely learned in some respects,
their culture on the whole (and the whole is really the flower
of wisdom) is incoherent. To avoid this serious drawback, I
would suggest that our professors should so co-ordinate all
disciplines into a single system so as to harmonize them with
our religion and with the spirit of the political form under
which we live. In this way, a coherent body of learning having
been established, it will be possible to teach it according to the
genius of our public polity.

XV

I have now set forth the remarks suggested to me by the
comparison of the study methods of our time with those of
antiquity, and by a confrontation of their respective advantages and disadvantages, so that our methods may be more
correct and finer in every respect.

If my ideas are true, I shall have reaped the supreme fruit

---

42 Antoine Favre (1557–1624) became famous for having pioneered in
that domain of juridical learning that is referred to as "interpolationist
research," i.e., for having pinpointed the alterations performed by the
compilers of Justinian's codification on the texts of the Roman jurists of
the "classical" epoch.

of my existence. It has been my constant effort, within the very limited range of my powers, to be useful to human society. But if my remarks should be considered false or lacking in practicality, my unquestionably honorable ambition and my earnest efforts towards a grand goal shall earn me a pardon.

It may be objected that, whereas facing danger when necessary is a sign of courage, undertaking a risk when there is no need of doing so is a sign of foolhardiness. "Why should you have undertaken to treat this subject which involves a knowledge of all sciences?"—some one will ask.

In answer, I will say: As G. B. Vico, I have no concern; but as a professor of eloquence, great concern in this undertaking. Our ancestors, the founders of this University, clearly showed, by assigning the professor of eloquence the task of delivering every year a speech exhorting our students to the study of the principles of various sciences and arts, that they felt he should be well versed in all fields of knowledge. Nor was it without reason that the great man, Bacon, when called upon to give advice to James, King of England, concerning the organization of a university, insisted that young scholars should not be admitted to the study of eloquence unless they had previously studied their way through the whole curriculum of learning.

What is eloquence, in effect, but wisdom, ornately and copiously delivered in words appropriate to the common opinion of mankind? Shall the professor of eloquence, to whom no student may have access unless previously trained in all sciences and arts, be ignorant of those subjects which are required by his teaching duties? The man who is deputed to exhort young students to grapple with all kinds of disciplines, and to discourse about their advantages and disadvantages, so that they may attain those and escape these, should he not be competent to expound his opinions on such knowledge?

For these reasons, teachers willing to bear this burden (a burden, I fear, vastly surpassing the strength of my shoulders) deserve to be likened, I feel, to C. Cilnius Maecenas, Crispus Sallustius, and other *equites illustres,* who, though possessed of financial means superior to those which the law prescribed for admission to senatorial rank, insisted on their wish to remain within the equestrian order. It was, therefore, not my duty alone as professor of eloquence, but my right as well to take up the subject of this discourse. What determined me was by no means the desire to diminish the prestige of a colleague or to place myself in the spotlight.

As you saw, whenever drawbacks had to be pointed out, I passed individual authors in silence; and whenever it was necessary to mention these authors, I did it with the utmost respect, since it was not for an unimportant man like me to censure persons so eminently great. As for the drawbacks, I sedulously set them forth as unobtrusively as possible.

From childhood, I have imposed on myself this rule (which the weakness of my fellow men has made a sacred one), to be as indulgent to the shortcomings of others as I would like others to be indulgent to my own, especially since others may have done many important things well, and failed only in a few cases, whereas I may have been guilty of countless errors in matters requiring but little ability.

In the present discourse, I have carefully refrained from any boasting; though my speech could have been pompously entitled "On the reconciliation of the study methods of antiquity with those of our time," I have preferred a more modest and usual designation. My purpose has been

> not to draw smoke from the brightness of light, but to bring out light from smokey murk.
>
> [Horace, *Ars poetica* 143]

I chose not to clothe my thought in high-sounding words, lest I should offend the intelligence of this assembly of listeners, every member of which knows how to reason with his own head and is fully conscious of his right to judge any author as he thinks best.

But, someone will object, "You were certainly bragging when you said that your theme was new." Not in the least. The fact that a theme is new is not automatically a recommendation; monstrous and ridiculous things may also be novelties. But to bring forward new things and to treat them in the right manner is unquestionably worthy of praise. Whether I did so, or not, I shall leave to the judgment of my listeners and to the common judgment of scholars, from whom, I vow, I shall never depart. In my life I have always had the greatest apprehension of being alone in wisdom; this kind of solitude exposes one to the danger of becoming either a god or a fool.

But, it will be urged, you have shown yourself thoroughly presumptuous in choosing a subject where you had to show a mastery of all learned disciplines and where you had to pass peremptory and pretentious judgment on them, as if you had been fully and deeply familiar with every one of them. To fend off the objection, I beg whosoever wants to press it to reflect on the kinds of judgments I have passed. Let him observe that a certain doctrine may be either beneficial or prejudicial to some persons; let him ascertain how the harm that such doctrine is likely to cause may be avoided. He will find out that judgment cannot be passed except by a man who has studied all of these matters, but

> of all these things, no one more deeply than all others,
> yet all of them indeed, in moderation.

[Terence, *The Lady of Andros* 58–59]

It is a common experience to see an individual who has concentrated all of his efforts on a single branch of study, and who has spent all his life on it, think that this field is, by far, more important than all others, and to see him inclined to make application of its specialty to matters wholly foreign to it. This may be due to the weakness of our nature, which prompts us to take an inordinate delight in ourselves and in our own pursuits.

Though I am afraid of delivering false judgments on all subjects, I am particularly afraid of advancing erroneous views on eloquence, since I profess it.

After stating this in defense of my assignment and of the

way I have discharged it, permit me to say that I shall be greatly indebted to any one who wishes to criticize with pertinence and with concrete reference to their intrinsic purport, the points that I have brought up, so as to free me from eventual errors. He will be certain to enlist my gratitude by his mere intent to do so.

APPENDIX

The Academies and the Relation
between Philosophy and Eloquence
1737

The Academies and the Relation
between Philosophy and Eloquence

TRANSLATED BY Donald Phillip Verene

[Vico delivered this address for the fourth annual inauguration of the Academy of Oziosi, meeting in January 1737 in the house of its influential patron and scholar, Nicola Maria Salerno (whom Vico refers to below as Niccolò Salerni). The Academy of Oziosi was one of a number of organizations of scholars which constituted much of the intellectual life of Naples during Vico's lifetime. Academies met to discuss literary, historical, and scientific matters and were involved, as is particularly true of the Academy of Oziosi, in the clash between conceptions of knowledge and learning as based on the eloquence of the Ancients versus the methodology of the sciences, the *veteres* against the *moderni*. Giambattista Manso founded the Academy of Oziosi at the beginning of the eighteenth century, and in 1733 a disciple of Vico, Giuseppe Pasquale Cirillo, revived the group with the help of other young scholars who shared Vico's ideas of knowledge and education. The Academy of Oziosi ceased in 1738, only one year after Vico's address. Vico's original Italian text appears in *Opere di Giambattista Vico*, vol. 6, ed. Giuseppe Ferrari (Milan: Società tipografica de' classici italiani, 1852), pp. 48–51, which was republished in *Opere di G. B. Vico*, vol. 7, ed. Fausto Nicolini (Bari: Laterza, 1940), pp. 33–37. The piece has no specific title. Ferrari entitled it simply "Discorso"; in the Laterza edition, Nicolini assigned it the title "Le accademie e i rapporti tra la filosofia e l'eloquenza." The style of the original depends upon an elaborate form of statement typical of such orations. The translation attempts to preserve this style and at the same time to render Vico's points as literally and clearly as possible.]

This name, "Academy," which we have taken from the Greeks to signify a community of scholars joined together for the purpose of exercising their powers of thought in works of erudition and learning, seems in regard to its origin to be suited to this most noble gathering more than to any other. Other academies have been instituted either for delivering discourses on special problems weighed in terms of an acute balancing of positions and counterpositions, or for considering particular topics of languages or scrutinizing particular experiments. But the Academy established by Socrates was a place where he, with elegance, copiousness, and ornament, reasoned about all parts of human and divine knowing; for this reason it is declared that the members of this Academy should, with cultivated, abundant, and ornate dissertations, course throughout all of the ample field of knowledge. Thus this Academy can rightfully call itself the one where Socrates reasoned.

This way of proceeding, above all, has the very great advantage that, although the noble spirits who gather here have applied themselves either for pleasure or for profession to a particular study of letters, thanks to such gatherings they succeed with time in acquiring all the cognitions necessary for an accomplished and wise thinker. Furthermore, and this is of very great importance, heart and language are here reunited in their natural bond, which Socrates, "full of philosophy in language[1] and breast," had firmly brought together. For beyond

---

[1] The term in the original is *lingua*, literally "tongue," as in *lingua materna*, "mother tongue," which combines with *petto*, "breast," to reinforce the physical sense of the image in this instance. Vico uses *lingua* throughout, which I have rendered as "language," but depending upon the context it can have the sense of "tongue" or "speech," what in French might be rendered as *parole*.

his school a violent divorce existed: the sophists exercised a vain art of speaking and the philosophers a dry and unadorned manner of understanding. Still other Greek "philosophizers," although of a nation as refined and noble as one could ever name or imagine, wrote in a language that was stretched like a very fine and pure veil of soft wax over the abstract forms of thought they conceived; and yet, although they had renounced ornament and copiousness in their philosophical argumentation, still they preserved elegance.

But when in the midst of the most robust barbarism there was a return to cultivating the ancient philosophies, which was given a beginning by Averroes' commentaries on the works of Aristotle, a kind of blind speaking was introduced, bereft of light, lacking in any softness of color, a cloying manner of reasoning, always in the same syllogistic form and quite spiritless gait, enumerating each order of discourse—*praemitto primo, praemitto secundo, obiicies primo, obiicies secundo.* Moreover, if I am not mistaken, I hold the opinion that if eloquence does not regain the luster of the Latins and Greeks in our time, when our sciences have made progress equal to and perhaps even greater than theirs, it will be because the sciences are taught completely stripped of every badge of eloquence. And, for all that Cartesian philosophy would claim to have corrected of the erroneous order of thought of which the Scholastics were guilty, placing the total force of its proofs in the geometric method, such a method is so subtle and drawn out that if by chance attention to one proposition is broken, it is completely lost to whoever is listening to comprehend anything of the whole of what is being said.

Yet Demosthenes came forth from the Platonic Academy where he had listened for a good eight years, and he came armed with his invincible enthymeme, which he formed by means of a very well regulated excess, going outside his case into quite distant things with which he tempered the lightning flashes of his arguments, which, when striking, amazed the listeners so much the more by how much he had diverted them. From the same Academy Cicero professed himself to be endowed with the felicity of his copiousness, which, like a great winter torrent, overflows banks, floods countrysides, crashes down over cliffs and hillsides, rolling before it heavy stones and ancient oaks; and triumphant over all that had given him resistance, he returns to the proper riverbed of his case.

It is of no use to defend our own small spirit (on account of which we pretend to be wholly spirit) by saying that Demosthenes and Cicero flourished in popular republics in which, as Tacitus says, eloquence and liberty are on a par.[2] In fact, the eloquence that Cicero had used in liberty was later employed before Caesar, ruler of Rome, on behalf of Quintus Ligarius.[3] In this case Cicero absolutely took the accused from Caesar's hands, he whom the dictator, on entering the Council, had himself openly professed to condemn, [later] saying these words: "Had Cicero not spoken so well today, Ligarius would not flee from our hands." In the sixteenth century, in which a well-spoken wisdom was celebrated, Giulio Camillo Delminio made tears come to the eyes of Francis I, King of France, with the oration he delivered for the liberation of his brother,[4] just as Monsignor Giovanni della Casa moved the Emperor Charles V with what he said to him for the return of Piacenza.[5] The oration on behalf of Ligarius is still the most glorious of all those of Cicero. He triumphed with language over him who with arms had tri-

---

[2] Tacitus, *Dialogus de oratoribus*, 36, 40–41; see also 32.

[3] Cicero, *Pro Ligario*.

[4] Giulio Camillo Delminio (1480–1544), one of the most famous figures of the sixteenth century, was known for his eloquence and his "memory theatre" described in his major work, *L'Idea del Theatro*, published at Florence and Venice in 1550, after his death. Concerning Camillo as orator, see *Due orationi di Giulio Camillo al Rè christianissimo* (Venice, 1545). On Camillo see Frances A. Yates, *The Art of Memory* (1966; Chicago: University of Chicago Press, 1974), chaps. 6–7; and Lina Bolzoni, *Il teatro della memoria: Studi su Giulio Camillo con un'appendice di tesi* (Padua: Liviana, 1984). Also see Lu Beery Wenneker, "An Examination of 'L'Idea del Theatro' of Giulio Camillo" (Ph.D. diss., University of Pittsburgh, 1970).

[5] Giovanni della Casa (1503–1556).

umphed over the whole world. Of the other two orations (the one delivered to a very great king, the other to a renowned emperor), the former is a queen and the latter is the empress of Tuscan orations.

Now to bring together in brief what has been said, you, *signori*, with masterful awareness, endeavor to employ in practice that precept of Horace which, condensed in three lines, contains all the art of using language well in prose as in verse.[6] "Right thinking is the first principle and source of writing," because there is no eloquence without truth and dignity; of these two parts wisdom is composed. "Socratic writings will direct you in the choice of subjects," that is, the study of morals, which principally informs the wisdom of man, to which more than in the other parts of philosophy Socrates divinely applied himself, whence of him it was said: "Socrates recalled moral philosophy from the heavens." And "when the subject is well conceived, words will follow on spontaneously," because of the natural bond by which we claim language and heart to be held fast together, for to every idea its proper voice stands naturally attached. Thus, eloquence is none other than wisdom speaking.

A good three years have now passed since this noble Academy, honorably received in this worthy place by Signor Don Niccolò Salerni, was founded; and with the same fervor with which it commenced, it happily continues against the malign course of foolish Fortune who cuts across beautiful enterprises and, being envious, she frequently overwhelms them in their earliest magnanimous efforts. Now, in this year you, in your generosity, beyond any I merit, wished and com-

---

[6] Horace, *Epistola ad Pisones* (*Ars Poetica*), 309–11. Vico quotes these lines in the original: "Scribendi recte sapere est et principium et fons: Rem tibi socraticae poterunt ostendere chartae, Verbaque provisam rem non invita sequentur." *Socraticae chartae*, i.e., writings of the followers of Socrates; Horace probably intends those of Plato, Xenophon, Aeschines, and perhaps Antisthenes. See also Vico's remarks, "L'epistola di Orazio ai Pisoni al lume della *Scienza nuova*" in *Opere di G. B. Vico*, ed. Fausto Nicolini (Bari: Laterza, 1911–41), 7:51–77.

manded me *custode* and colleague of Signor de Canosa (with whose most noble personage this community is adorned),[7] having appointed Signor Don Paolo Doria censor, a mind of rare and sublime intelligence and most celebrated for many works of philosophy and mathematics among the learned of his age.[8] And, by way of overwhelming me with highest and sovereign honor, he commanded that I make the annual opening address.

Therefore, having collected all my powers in a thought of highest reverence, the formula being dictated to me by the great Father Augustine, under whose protection this Academy stands resigned, I conceived this prayer with these solemn and consecrated words—Hear, humbly I pray you, hear, not fabulous Minerva, but Eternal Wisdom, generated from the divine head of the true Jove, the omnipotent Your Father.[9] Today in Your praise, in Your honor, in Your glory is reopened this fourth Academy year, that it might be for the perfection of these well-born intelligences, because wisdom, which is mind and language, is the perfecter of man in his properly being man.

---

[7] Nicolini quotes the following from the catalogue of the society for 1731: "Fabrizio Minutolo principe di Canosa, custode; Giambattista Vico, regio professore ordinario di eloquenza nell'Università di Napoli, custode; Paolo Mattia Doria de' principi d'Angri, censore" (see Nicolini's annotations to the oration, *Opere*, 7:265).

[8] Paolo Mattia Doria (1667–1746) was Vico's lifelong friend and supporter to whom he dedicated *De antiquissima Italorum sapientia* (1710). Among Doria's prolific writings are his attack on Cartesianism, *Discorsi critici filosofici intorno alla filosofia degl'antichi e dei moderni* (1724), which was followed by his attack on Locke, *Difesa della metafisica degli antichi contro il signor Giovanni Locke* (2 vols., 1732–33). Doria's unpublished works have been collected in *Monoscritti napoletani di Paolo Mattia Doria*, 5 vols., ed. G. Belgioioso et al. (Galatina: Congedo, 1981–82).

[9] Cf. Augustine, *Confessions*, I.1; *City of God*, VII.29. Vico here selects St. Augustine from among the saints who were protectors of the Academy of Oziosi, the others being St. Jerome, St. Thomas Aquinas, and St. Teresa. In signing his third set of "Corrections, Meliorations, and Additions" to the 1730 edition of the *New Science*, Vico calls St. Augustine his "particular protector" (*particolare protettore*). See *Opere*, 5:377.

Library of Congress Cataloging-in-Publication Data

Vico, Giambattista, 1668–1744.
  [De nostri temporis studiorum ratione. English]
  On the study methods of our time / Giambattista Vico ; translated, with
an introduction and notes, by Elio Gianturco ; preface by Donald Phillip
Verene ; with a translation of The academies and the relation between phi-
losophy and eloquence by Donald Phillip Verene.
    p. cm.
  Translation of: De nostri temporis studiorum ratione.
  Vico's oration translated from the Italian.
  Rev. and enl. version of the ed. published by Bobbs-Merrill, 1965, with
new preface, appendix, and chronology of Vico's writings.
  Includes bibliographical references.
  ISBN 0-8014-2543-3 (alk. paper).—ISBN 0-8014-9778-7 (pbk. : alk. pa-
per)
  1. Education, Higher. 2. Education—Philosophy. I. Vico, Giambattista,
1668-1744. Accademie e i rapporti tra la filosofia e l'eloquenza.
English. 1990. II. Title.
LB575.V5D413   1990
370'.1—dc20
                                       90-55226